Underwriting Principles

Underwriting Principles

Joseph F. Mangan, CPCU
Insurance Consultant

Connor M. Harrison, CPCU, AU
Director of Underwriting Education
Insurance Institute of America

Second Edition • 2000

Insurance Institute of America, 720 Providence Road, Malvern, Pennsylvania 19355-0770

Foreword

The American Institute for Chartered Property Casualty Underwriters and the Insurance Institute of America are independent, nonprofit, educational organizations serving the needs of the property and liability insurance business. The Institutes develop a wide range of curricula, study materials, and examinations in response to the educational requirements of various elements of the business.

The American Institute confers the Chartered Property Casualty Underwriter (CPCU®) professional designation on those who meet the Institute's experience, ethics, and examination requirements. The Insurance Institute of America offers associate designations and certificate programs in the following technical and managerial fields:

- Accounting and Finance
- Agent and Producer Studies
- Claims
- Information Technology
- Insurance Fundamentals
- International Risk Management and Insurance
- Management Studies
- Marine Insurance
- Personal Lines
- Premium Auditing
- Quality Service
- Regulation and Compliance
- Reinsurance
- Risk Management
- Surety Bonds and Crime Insurance
- Surplus Lines
- Underwriting

The *Writing at Work* course offers people an opportunity to improve their written communication skills. Through the Institutes' *Focus Series*® of topical presentations, often accepted for continuing education (CE) credit, students can concentrate on a single subject. The Institutes are committed to developing new and innovative risk management and insurance educational products and services to meet the evolving needs of the business world.

The Center for the Advancement of Risk Management Education (CARME), a division of the Institutes, serves as the focal point for the Institutes' risk management programs:

- Introduction to Risk Management
- Associate in Risk Management (ARM)
- Risk Management for Public Entities
- Focus Series: Risk Management for Insurance Professionals

The Insurance Institute for Applied Ethics was established in 1995 to heighten awareness of the pervasiveness of ethical decision making in insurance and to explore ways to raise the level of ethical behavior among parties to the insurance contract. The Ethics Institute sponsors seminars and workshops on the role of ethics in the insurance transaction. It also identifies and funds practical research projects on ethics-related topics and publishes the findings. In addition, it produces booklets, newsletters, and videotapes on ethics issues.

The Insurance Research Council (IRC) was established in 1977 as an independent, not-for-profit research institute to examine public policy issues that affect property and liability insurers and their customers. In 1998, the IRC merged with the American Institute for CPCU and became a division of the Institutes. The IRC provides timely and reliable information based on extensive data collection and analyses and conducts empirical studies on a wide range of topics relating to all lines of property and liability insurance. IRC research reports are widely distributed to assist the public and insurers in reaching sound decisions on legislative and regulatory matters. The IRC is devoted solely to research and the communication of its research findings.

The Institutes began publishing textbooks in 1976. Since then, we have produced more than ninety individual textbook volumes. Despite the vast differences in the subjects and purposes of these volumes, they all have much in common. First, each book is specifically designed to increase knowledge and develop skills that can improve job performance and help students achieve the educational objectives of the course for which it is assigned. Second, all of the manuscripts for our texts are widely reviewed before publication, by both insurance business practitioners and members of the academic community. In addition, the revisions of our texts often incorporate improvements that students and course leaders suggested.

We welcome criticisms of and suggestions for improving our publications. It is only with such constructive comments that we can improve the quality of our study materials. Please direct any comments you may have on this text to the Curriculum Department of the Institutes.

Terrie E. Troxel, Ph.D., CPCU, CLU
President and CEO

Preface

Underwriting Principles provides the reader with an understanding of underwriting fundamentals that is useful to commercial underwriters.

Underwriting Principles is written for students working toward the Insurance Institute of America's Associate in Underwriting (AU) designation. The required courses for this designation are listed below, with the texts that each requires.

- CPCU 3—Commercial Property Insurance and Risk Management; *Commercial Property Insurance and Risk Management*, volumes 1 and 2
- CPCU 4—Commercial Liability Insurance and Risk Management; *Commercial Liability Insurance and Risk Management*, volumes 1 and 2
- AU 65—Commercial Underwriting: Principles and Property; *Underwriting Principles and Underwriting Commercial Property*
- AU 66—Commercial Underwriting: Liability and Advanced Techniques; *Underwriting Principles and Underwriting Commercial Property*

Although there is no required course sequence, we recommend that students have an understanding of commercial coverages before taking the underwriting courses. Studying and preparing for CPCU 3 and CPCU 4 can provide such an understanding, as can completing the commercial coverage course in the Program in General Insurance: INS 23—Commerical Insurance.

The contents of Underwriting Principles can be summarized as follows:

- Chapter 1 serves as an introduction to underwriting. Underwriters implement insurers' underwriting policy through individual risk selection. Because underwriters perform tasks other than risk selection, it is often convenient to categorize these tasks as those performed by line underwriters and those performed by staff underwriters. The success of insurer underwriting activities are usually measured by its combined ratio, which indicates whether premiums collected are adequate to pay losses and loss adjustment expenses. This chapter also introduces an underwriting process that should serve inexperienced underwriters with an approach—not a formula—to making better underwriting decisions.

- Chapter 2 describes the organization of business enterprises and the general underwriting concerns of insuring them. The type of business ownership, caliber of management, and use of employees or independent contractors all present issues the underwriter must evaluate. This chapter concludes with the introduction of a widely used business classification system that underwriters sometimes use to place the operations of a particular account into context.

- Chapter 3 describes the sources of information available to underwriters for account selection decision making. Underwriters usually base their decision to write an account on the information provided on the insurance application and on that provided by the agent or broker submitting the account. Sometimes, underwriters need additional information such as that provided on a loss control report or that received from financial reporting services. Insurers usually stress to their underwriters that they should obtain only information that is absolutely necessary for the risk selection decision.

- Chapter 4 describes financial statements and how underwriters can use financial analysis of financial statements to evaluate an account. An account's fiscal well-being is often used as a proxy for measuring subjective factors that reflect management quality. Ratio analysis can be used by underwriters to determine whether the account is performing better than or worse than the account's respective industry norm.

- Chapter 5 describes the underwriter's role in pricing the insurance product. Underwriters are often under pressure to increase market share by insuring more accounts while retaining existing ones. Underwriters might modify insurance rates—which should be adequate, not excessive, and not unfairly discriminatory, so that the insurer's overall book of business becomes inadequately priced. If an insurer's book of business is under-priced, the long-term solvency of the insurer might be threatened.

The authors would like to recognize and thank the following groups of people who have reviewed and commented on the manuscript of this text.

The advisory committee for the Associate in Underwriting program serves as the Institutes' primary connection to the educational needs of commercial underwriters. In addition to its role of shaping the curriculum, this committee assists in the development of the national examination. The members of this committee are listed below.

Margaret A. Ball, CPCU, AU, AMIM, ARe
Senior Vice President
Employers Mutual Companies

Roger P. Carlson, CPCU, AU, ARM, AIM
Director, Underwriting
St. Paul Fire and Marine Insurance Company

James W. Gow, Jr., CPCU, AU
Division Vice President
Fireman's Fund

Joseph L. Grauwiler, CPCU
Vice President, Corporate Underwriting
National Grange Mutual Insurance Company

Frederick R. Parcells, CPCU, ARM, ARe
Senior Specialty Executive Underwriter
Interstate Insurance Group

Jon A. Rhodes, CPCU, ARM
Vice President, Underwriting
The Central Companies

Deborah K. Ropelewski, CPCU, AU, ARM, ARe, CPIW
Vice President
Healthcare Risk Service, Inc.

William M. Tarbell, CPCU, AU, ARM, AFSB, ARe
Vice President, Commercial Underwriting
Providence Washington Insurance Company

Few people know the content of the AU texts better than those who grade the national examinations do. In addition to their personal knowledge of commercial underwriting, which they share during the grading process, the graders have served as the primary reviewers of this text. The AU grading panel is listed below.

Sheryl A. Feigenberg, AU, AAI
Commercial Lines Account Manager
Clair Odell Group

John P. Ferry, CPCU, CLU, AU, ARM, AIM
Senior Claims Representative
Travelers Insurance Group

James W. Gow, Jr. CPCU, AU
Division Vice President
Fireman's Fund

Richard E. Hess, AU
Managing Director – Marketing
Chester County Mutual Insurance Company

Peter J. Tyler, CPCU, AU, ARM, AAM
Senior Technical Specialist
CGU Insurance

Thomas P. Weiant, CPCU, AU
Commercial Underwriter
Accordia of Pennsylvania

Many AU graduates and AU instructors took an active role in reviewing and rewriting the manuscripts. We are deeply indebted to their continued commitment to the Institutes and the insurance underwriting profession. These people are listed below.

Shelly J. Arnold, CPCU, AAI, ARM, AU, ACSR, CPIW
Executive Vice President
Independent Insurance Agents of Maryland

John R. Chesebrough, CPCU, CLU, ChFC, AU, AIM, ARM
Insurance Consultant
Chesebrough Associates

Sheila E. Coleman
Large Accounts Coordinator
Berkshire Hathaway Homestate Companies

Richard Fox, CPCU, ARM, ALCM, AIM
Commercial Underwriting Supervisor
Harleysville Insurance Companies

Paul Mandt, CPCU, CIC, ARM, AU
Training, Research and Development
Farmers Union Service Association, Ltd.

Anne E. Myhr, CPCU, ARM, AU, AIM
Training Consultant
ACE USA

Leigh A. Polhill, CPCU, AU, CPIW
Commercial Lines Underwriting Manager
Seibels, Bruce and Co.

David Rispoli, CPCU, AU
Insurance Agent
Hampson Mowrer Kreitz Agency

James "Skip" Spencer, AIAF
Research Analyst
Hastings Mutual Insurance Company

Gregg Talmage, CPCU, AU
Senior Commercial Lines Underwriter
Lake States Insurance Company

Jerry E. Tuttle, FCAS, FCIA, CPCU, ARM, ARe, AIM
Vice President—Senior Pricing Officer
St. Paul Re

Several members of the Institute staff had a role in this revision and are listed below.

Lowell S. Young, CPCU, CLU, APA, ASLI, AIAF, ARC, Director of Curriculum, provided a comprehensive review of the exhibits used in the text. Lowell made several suggestions that improved the accuracy and clarity of the exhibits.

Kenneth N. Scoles Jr., Ph.D., AIAF, Director of Curriculum, reviewed the manuscript for Chapter 4—Financial Analysis. Ken updated the financial statements and coordinated the text's discussion with that of CPCU 8—Accounting and Finance.

Arthur L. Flitner, CPCU, ARM, AIC, Assistant Vice President & Senior Director of Curriculum Design, provided suggestions that resulted in the restructuring of this edition. Arthur reviewed every chapter, and his contributions to the improvement of the text appear throughout.

Kathleen Q. Spicciati, Production Manager/Inventory Coordinator, edited the manuscripts for this text and led the team that produced it. Students should especially appreciate Kathy's contribution to the text as she focused on improving the clarity and readability of the text.

Connor M. Harrison
Joseph F. Mangan

Contents

Chapter 1

Fundamentals of Underwriting

Underwriting is the process of (1) deciding which accounts are acceptable; (2) determining the premiums to be charged and the terms and conditions of the insurance contract, and (3) monitoring each of those decisions. Yet underwriting can also be viewed in a broader context. Underwriting is what insurers do to be financially successful. From an organizational perspective, underwriting is more than the risk selection task performed by individual underwriters; underwriting determines which products the insurer will sell and to whom.

Underwriting is crucial to an insurer's success. Favorable underwriting results are necessary for the profitable growth—even the survival—of the insurer. Although most insurer organizations include other specialty areas, such as actuarial, claims, and marketing, all insurer activities follow from corporate underwriting decisions.

This text, *Underwriting Principles*, provides a foundation for underwriting study. The topics selected for this text should provide the reader with an overview of underwriting and an understanding of the basic skills required of a commercial underwriter.

This chapter examines the purpose of underwriting and how most property-liability insurers are organized to conduct their underwriting activities. Additionally, this chapter describes an underwriting process that an underwriter can follow in making sound decisions.

> **How Underwriters Got Their Name**
> By the end of the seventeenth century, individuals interested in outfitting voyages or investing in such ventures often gathered at Edward Lloyd's Coffee House on Lombard Street near the Royal Exchange in London. It became customary for those gathered there to arrange mutual contracts of insurance against the perils of the sea to which their ventures were exposed. When notices of prospective voyages appeared describing the ship, its cargo, master crew, and destination, individuals *wrote* their names and the amount of liability they would assume *under* the description of those voyages they were willing to insure. For this reason, those insuring a voyage became known as *underwriters*.[1]

The Purpose of Underwriting

Insurance has been defined as "a system by which a risk is transferred by a person, business, or organization to an insurance company, which reimburses the insured for covered losses and provides for the sharing of the costs of losses among all insureds."[2] The purpose of underwriting is to ensure that the risk transfer is equitable and the insurer is able to develop and maintain a growing, profitable book of business.

> **Book of Business**
> Book of business is insurance industry terminology that refers to the collection of all the policies written by an insurer. This term is also used to refer to a subset of the insurer's policies. For example, an insurer might refer to its "commercial general liability book of business" or its "Alabama book of business." Similarly, an insurer might refer to the insurance produced by an agent as that agent's "book of business." Because this term can have various meanings, this text will use it to refer to all of an insurer's policies unless its use is otherwise qualified.

Experience has proven that insurers cannot accept every applicant for insurance. People who have a greater-than-average exposure to loss generally want insurance more than those who have relatively little exposure to loss do. Insurers refer to this phenomenon as **adverse selection**. If an insurer were to accept too many of these higher-risk applicants, the premium would prove to be inadequate and insurance rates would have to increase. Insureds who are *not* so high-risk would not be willing to pay the higher premium and would therefore move their insurance coverage to another insurer. Eventually, the rates charged to the high-risk insureds would be too great even for them to tolerate. In this situation, the insurer will not be able to raise its rates fast enough to pay for the losses incurred. Not only will the insurer fail to meet its goal of earning a profit, the insurer will likely become insolvent and go out of business.

Conversely, insurers that are too selective will be unable to meet their growth goals. Therefore, insurers must strike a balance between their objectives of growth and profitability. Insurers employ underwriters, professional risk takers, to select accounts that satisfy the goals established by the insurer's management.

In insurance organizations today, underwriting responsibilities are delegated by members of senior management to others. The section that follows describes a common dichotomy—staff versus line—that is used to distinguish between management-level underwriting activities and underwriting activities of people making the day-to-day risk-selection decisions. For many insurers, staff underwriting activities are performed by insurer personnel who would not necessarily be classified as "staff underwriters."

Underwriting Activities

There is no *one* way to organize insurer-underwriting activities. However, as mentioned above, many insurers make a distinction between line and staff underwriting activities. **Staff underwriting activities** are underwriting management activities that are aimed at managing the risk selection process and that are often delegated to specialists within the underwriting department. **Line underwriting activities** are those directed at evaluating new submissions and renewal underwriting. However, in some companies, a single underwriter might have both line and staff underwriting responsibilities.

How an insurer's underwriting activities are organized is often a reflection of the decision-making authority granted to individual underwriters. Physical location of individual underwriters—home office versus branch office—once required that decision-making autonomy be granted when referral to others was not practical. For many insurers, information systems have made underwriting referrals from remote offices to the home office possible. The delegation of underwriting authority is an important concern, and its discussion concludes this section.

Staff Underwriting Activities

Although staff underwriting activities are usually performed at the home office, some regional underwriting managers have staff assistants. The major staff underwriting activities are as follows:

- Formulating underwriting policy
- Assisting others with complex accounts
- Evaluating loss experience
- Developing coverage forms
- Reviewing and revising pricing plans
- Preparing underwriting guidelines
- Arranging treaty reinsurance
- Conducting underwriting audits
- Participating in industry associations
- Conducting education and training

The following sections describe each of these activities.

Formulating Underwriting Policy

Underwriting policy, sometimes referred to as an insurer's **underwriting philosophy**, guides individual and aggregate decision making. Underwriting policy should support the insurer's mission statement. A **mission statement** is usually a broad expression of an entity's goals. For most insurers, underwriting policy translates those goals into specific strategies that, in turn, determine the composition of the insurer's book of business. Underwriting policy is communicated through written manuals usually referred to as **underwriting guidelines** or the **underwriting guide**.

Staff underwriters formulate and implement underwriting policy. Formulating underwriting policy might require staff underwriters to evaluate and reevaluate market-related questions such as the following:

- What insurance products should be sold?
- What type of accounts or classifications should be pursued?
- Which states should be expanded into or withdrawn from?
- What is the ideal mix of insurance products?
- What are the premium-volume goals?

For most insurers, staff underwriters work with staff members from other departments in formulating underwriting policy. Actuarial, claim, loss control, and marketing departments each have responsibilities so closely tied to those of the underwriting department that their involvement is needed in most changes to underwriting policy. Cooperation and collaboration of insurer departments is needed for optimal underwriting-policy formulation.

Insurer Functions

Claim. The primary function of the **claim department** is to investigate claims and satisfy the obligations of the insurer to the policyholder as agreed to in the insurance policy. Judicious operation of the claim department is essential if the insurer is to satisfy its profit objectives.

Actuarial. Actuaries are trained in applying mathematical techniques to insurer operations. The **actuarial department** performs (1) ratemaking, (2) verification of loss reserves, (3) collection and analysis of insurer loss data to evaluate insurer profitability, (4) analysis of data from other sources to determine the insurer's competitive position, and (5) preparation of statistical reports for management and regulatory authorities.

Marketing. The **marketing department** is responsible for identifying new marketing opportunities, developing new products, and measuring success in reaching those markets. Traditionally, many of these responsibilities are directed by staff underwriters in cooperation with other departments. For many insurers, direct contact with the insurer's agency force is managed through the agency department that performs many of the insurer's marketing functions. An insurer's marketing efforts are generally linked to the distribution system it uses.

Loss control. The **loss control department**, often part of an insurer's underwriting department, is responsible for inspecting the premises and operations of those who apply for insurance. **Loss control representatives**, the individuals who physically visit the account, provide information to underwriters to help them make better decisions. For many accounts, the loss control representative can make recommendations that will improve the underwriting profitability of the account.

Premium auditing. The **premium audit department** is responsible for examining the financial records of insureds whose premiums are based on variable exposure bases, such as payroll or receipts. **Premium auditors** often perform **field audits** (also referred to as **physical audits**), but for some accounts they work with information provided by the insured, which is called a **voluntary report**.

Reinsurance. The **reinsurance department** negotiates and manages reinsurance agreements and individual transactions with reinsurers. Sometimes, staff underwriters perform these tasks.

No single underwriting policy is appropriate for all insurers. Many insurers seek what they consider to be better-than-average accounts for which the average premium is more than adequate. These insurers generally view themselves as serving the "standard market." Other insurers market their products (coverages) to higher-risk applicants, whom they can charge a higher-than-average premium. A variety of terms are used to refer to the insurance market for worse-than-average accounts, but this text will refer to it as the "nonstandard market." There are also accounts that have unique needs that are not adequately addressed in the standard market. These insurance needs, such as professional liability, are often met in the "specialty market." Insurers often view themselves and develop their underwriting policy within the context of the markets they serve.

Underwriting policy is central to controlling an insurer's account selection activities. After this chapter concludes its discussion of underwriting activities, it will discuss the parameters affecting underwriting policy and approaches to implementing underwriting policy. Additionally, designing underwriting policy is discussed in greater detail in *Advanced Underwriting Techniques*.[3]

Assisting Others With Complex Accounts

Staff underwriters often serve as consultants to other underwriters. Generally, staff underwriters have significant first-hand line underwriting experience. Additionally, as "referral underwriters," they see complex and atypical accounts regularly that most line underwriters see only occasionally.

Evaluating Loss Experience

Staff underwriters evaluate insurer loss experience to determine whether changes should be made in underwriting guidelines. Insurers, of course, anticipate losses, and underwriting management usually has expectations as to what the level of losses should be. Insurance products that have excessive losses—greater than those anticipated—are usually targeted for analysis. Staff underwriters research loss data to determine the specific source of the excess losses. Part of this research includes an analysis of insurance industry loss experience that might reveal trends affecting the insurer's products. Based on their evaluation, staff underwriters, usually with the agreement of other key departments, make adjustments to the insurer's underwriting guidelines.

Developing Coverage Forms

Staff underwriters usually work cooperatively with the actuarial and legal departments to develop new coverages. As in other businesses, insurers develop new coverages to meet changing consumer needs. Additionally, insurers modify existing coverages so that the coverage being provided by the insurer will respond as anticipated. An unfavorable court decision, for example, might cause an insurer to rewrite a coverage form to limit the coverage being provided. Competition from insurers that have broader coverage forms often drives insurer product development.

Insurance advisory organizations have a significant role in the development of commonly used—"standard"—coverage forms. Insurance advisory organization-developed coverage forms are usually developed by coverage experts who consider the grant of coverage being provided, coverage provided by the insured's other policies, and legal restrictions that apply to coverage-form development. Because insurance advisory organization forms are used widely, the courts usually identify ambiguous policy language or other problems with the coverage form.

Staff underwriters of participating insurers might be asked to serve on an insurance advisory organization committee that reviews coverage language and recommends changes. The current trend toward the deregulation of commercial lines of insurance, however, might reduce the demand for and importance of insurance advisory organization-developed coverage forms and increase the use of insurer-developed coverage forms.

> ### Commercial Lines Deregulation
> Several states have enacted laws that lift the filing requirements applicable to rates and forms for large commercial insureds, with the general exception of workers compensation insurance. Until recently, and in most states, insurers have had to submit their rates, rules, and forms to state insurance regulators for approval. Insurers will benefit from decreased filing requirements because doing so will give them needed flexibility to write large accounts that often move their insurance to offshore and alternative markets.

Reviewing and Revising Pricing Plans

Pricing plans and coverage forms are usually developed together. As they do with coverage form development, staff underwriters usually work with their counterparts in the actuarial department to ensure that the insurer is adequately compensated for the coverage it provides. Production efficiencies or a superior account-selection process can lead to a pricing plan that provides the insurer with a competitive advantage.

As with coverage form development, many insurers belong to insurance advisory organizations (at one time referred to as "rating bureaus") that gather insurance industry data so individual insurers can perform ratemaking. The role of insurance advisory organizations was challenged in the 1980s as being anticompetitive, and the practice of calculating "final rates" was generally discontinued. Now, insurance advisory organizations gather historical data and develop prospective loss costs. **Prospective loss costs** are simply loss data that have been modified by necessary loss development, trending, and credibility processes—not including insurer profit and expenses. Insurers combine prospective loss costs with an insurer-developed profit and expense loading to create a final rate used in policy pricing.

Insurance Advisory Organizations

An **insurance advisory organization** is an organization formed to assist its members and subscribers in gathering the data necessary to calculate rates. The role of the insurance advisory organization continues to evolve in response to regulatory and consumer-group pressure. The primary insurance advisory organizations are Insurance Services Office, the National Council on Compensation Insurance, and the American Association of Insurance Services.

Insurance Services Office (ISO) is the leading supplier of statistical, actuarial, and underwriting information for and about the property-liability insurance industry. ISO provides advisory services to more than 1,500 participating insurers and their agents. ISO is licensed to perform these services throughout the United States, including Puerto Rico. ISO's core products include projections of expected claims, standardized policy contract language, underwriting rules, and property surveys. ISO reports quarterly and annually on industry financial operating results and produces research studies on issues affecting the industry. [4]

The **National Council on Compensation Insurance (NCCI)** is the preeminent influence on the administration of workers compensation insurance. The NCCI is a shared service, not-for-profit corporation that provides products and services to insurers writing workers compensation insurance. In thirty-two states and the District of Columbia, the NCCI is the licensed rating bureau operating under the laws of the state. Other states have independent bureaus that rely on actuarial and statistical services provided by the NCCI or that closely follow the methods of the NCCI. Even in states with monopolistic state funds for workers compensation insurance, the NCCI may provide advisory services. The NCCI serves its member companies by providing ratemaking and regulatory services, experience rating and other risk services, and residual market management. Additionally, the NCCI monitors social, economic, and regulatory trends to analyze the potential effect on the workers compensation system. [5]

The **American Association of Insurance Services (AAIS)** is an incorporated association of insurance companies. The AAIS functions as both a rating organization and statistical agent in all states. As a licensed advisory organization, the AAIS develops, maintains, and files rates, rules, and policy forms for fourteen property and casualty lines of insurance.[6]

Preparing Underwriting Guidelines

Staff underwriters are usually responsible for revising underwriting guidelines so that they accurately reflect changes in underwriting policy. Underwriting guidelines, which are generally used to distinguish what accounts the insurer deems acceptable and unacceptable, will be discussed in more detail later in this chapter.

Arranging Treaty Reinsurance

A nontechnical definition of **reinsurance** is that it is "insurance for insurers." Reinsurance is a way for insurers to transfer risk to other insurers. **Treaty reinsurance** is a contractual arrangement between insurers to transfer risk on an ongoing basis for a specific insurance product or products. **Facultative reinsurance**, in contrast, is a risk transfer agreement applicable to a single account. Line underwriters arrange for facultative reinsurance when characteristics of the account—limits requested or account classification—make it unsuitable for inclusion under the insurer's treaty reinsurance program.

Treaty reinsurance is an indispensable aspect of underwriting management. The responsibility for securing and maintaining treaty reinsurance usually belongs to staff underwriters. Their responsibility includes determining the insurer's needs for reinsurance, selecting reinsurers, negotiating the terms and conditions of reinsurance treaties, and maintaining the insurer's relations with its treaty reinsurers. The availability of treaty reinsurance can exert a significant influence on the insurer's appetite for risk, as measured by the volatility of the lines of business written and the coverage limits the insurer will provide.

For many insurers, treaty reinsurance limitations are directly reflected in their underwriting guidelines. Underwriting guidelines might, for example, specify the maximum coverage limits that can be offered because higher limits of treaty reinsurance were not purchased. Additionally, some types of accounts cannot be insured because the insurer's treaty reinsurance agreements specifically exclude the account's classification. For commercial property accounts, many insurers maintain a **line authorization guide**, which serves as a control on the property limits accepted.

Conducting Underwriting Audits

Staff underwriters are often responsible for monitoring line underwriter activities and do so by conducting underwriting audits. **Underwriting audits** are on-site reviews of selected underwriting files to ensure that individual underwriters are adhering to the practices and procedures outlined in the underwriting guidelines. Underwriting audits usually focus on the paper trail of the insurance transaction from the insurance application to the issued policy.

Participating in Industry Associations

Many insurers are members of national and state associations that address insurance industry concerns. Additionally, insurers often share in the operating of residual market mechanisms, such as automobile joint underwriting associations and windstorm pools. Staff underwriters typically represent the insurer as a member of these organizations.

Conducting Education and Training

Staff underwriters are usually responsible for determining the education and training needs of line underwriters. Sometimes, these training needs are addressed through a formal training program that all newly hired underwriters must complete. At other times, the training need is transitory and is provided through classes that address a specific underwriting issue or procedure. Although some training needs are met through programs provided by the insurer's human resources department, staff underwriters usually provide technical insurance education.

Line Underwriting Activities

Line underwriters, often referred to as **desk underwriters**, evaluate individual accounts for acceptability. Line underwriters execute underwriting policy by following practices and procedures outlined in the underwriting guidelines. The specific tasks line underwriters perform may vary by insurer; however, most line underwriters are responsible for the following activities:

- Selection of insureds
- Classification of accounts
- Providing requested coverage
- Determination of the appropriate price
- Service to producers and policyholders
- Management of books of business
- Marketing support

In addition to the preceding activities, some line underwriters also analyze insurance needs, design insurance coverages, and set rates. The following sections provide an overview of the major activities of line underwriters.

Selection of Insureds

Line underwriters select insureds that meet the criteria established by the insurer. As mentioned previously, active selection of insureds is essential for the insurer to avoid adverse selection by insurance applicants. The commercial success of insurance is due in part to the operation of the law of large numbers. One of the criteria for the *ideal* operation of the law of large numbers is that insureds be selected randomly. However, in reality, without the selection activity of the line underwriter, accounts with a higher-than-average chance of loss would be charged an inadequate premium. Furthermore, line underwriters usually attempt to select *superior accounts*—those that are better than average—for which the premium charged will be more than adequate.

The Law of Large Numbers

Insureds transfer risk to insurers. A building's owners, for example, have no idea whether their building will suffer a loss during any given year. An insurer, on the other hand, has pooled risk from thousands of insureds and is certain that some losses will occur. The accuracy of the insurer's loss prediction increases as the size of the pool increases. This is how the law of large numbers operates to make risk transference commercially feasible. Chapter 5 of this text will discuss the law of large numbers in more detail and describe conditions that increase the likelihood of its successful operation.

Line underwriting selection activities are ongoing. Line underwriters monitor accounts to ensure that they *continue* to be acceptable. A line underwriter might cancel or nonrenew an account if loss control recommendations made at the policy's inception are not implemented or if the insured fails to take corrective action to control loss frequency.

"Account selection" invokes a negative connotation because it involves discriminating among accounts. Line underwriters, however, should recognize the importance of this task. Effective account selection allows insurance to be commercially viable. Account selection enables insurers to ration their available capacity to obtain an optimum spread of loss exposures by location, class, size of risk, and line of business.

Classification of Accounts

Account classification is the process of grouping accounts with similar attributes so they can be priced appropriately. Line underwriters are responsible for ensuring that all the information needed for classification is obtained.

In many insurance companies, line underwriters do not personally perform either the classification or the pricing task. Line underwriters, however, are accountable for the correct accomplishment of these activities. As readers will find in *Underwriting Commercial Property*[7] and *Underwriting Commercial Liability*,[8] the process of account classification and pricing involves so many nuances that line underwriters really cannot completely relegate this task to others.

A consequence of misclassification is that the premium charged is not commensurate with the risk transferred. Accounts that are misclassified and priced too low receive a bargain but at the expense of the insurer. Insureds might move accounts that are charged too much because of a misclassification to another insurer once the insured discovers a better price. Insurers submit classification plans—as well as rates and forms—to state insurance regulators. Insurers who do not implement their classification plan as filed are subject to possible fines.

Providing Requested Coverage

Line underwriters have a role in ensuring that accounts obtain the coverage they request. Determining an insured's coverage needs is generally the responsibility of the insurance agent or broker or the insured's risk manager. The sophistication of insureds varies, and some insureds choose to treat many of their loss exposures with risk management techniques other than insurance. Many insureds select an alternative risk treatment for some exposures but choose to use insurance for other exposures. Line underwriters often inquire about an insured's risk management program to ensure that they are using other risk management techniques to address gaps in insurance coverage.

The task of providing requested coverage often involves collaboration between the producer and the line underwriter. Because each account is unique, producers and risk managers often want to know how coverage will respond to a specific type of loss. Line underwriters can respond to these requests by explaining the types of losses the coverage forms are designed to cover and the endorsements that must be added to provide the coverage desired. For some complex or unique accounts, the line underwriter, if sufficiently trained to do so, will draft a **manuscript policy** or endorsement worded to address the specific coverage needs of the insured. For most accounts, however, the line underwriter simply ensures that the policy is being issued with the appropriate forms and endorsements that provide the requested coverage.

Determination of the Appropriate Price

Line underwriters are responsible for ensuring that accounts are priced properly. Insurer rating manuals contain procedures that specify how to develop premiums for most coverages. **Underwriting technicians**, specialists in policy pricing and issuance preparation, usually perform the mechanics of pricing. Because most insurance is sold based on the policy's price alone, line underwriters participate to some extent in the pricing process.

The appropriate price charged must not only be adequate to permit the insurer to continue to write profitable business, but also competitive with the prices of other insurers. For some lines of business and in some states, line underwriters might not have any discretionary latitude in policy pricing. In other lines of insurance, the line underwriter can use individual rating plans to apply debits and credits to the account that will adjust the premium to reflect the characteristics of the individual insured. The line underwriter must be sure that the account characteristics justify the adjustment and must document that it is in accordance with the insurer's individual rating plan filed with regulatory authorities. Individual rating plans, which permit some pricing flexibility, are discussed in Chapter 5.

Service to Producers and Insureds

The services that line underwriters are expected to provide to producers and insureds vary by insurer. Some insurers rely on customer service departments to respond to routine inquiries and requests. Insurers operating through independent agents often rely on their sales force to perform many policy service functions. Because customer service activities and underwriting are often interwoven, line underwriters have an active interest in ensuring that producers' and insureds' needs are met.

Line underwriters are usually directly involved with producers in the preparation of policy quotations. Agents and brokers devote significant time and expense to prospecting new accounts. This effort is lost if the insurer develops a quote that will not "win" the account. In today's highly competitive market, producers want to deal with decisive line underwriters who respond quickly and demonstrate flexibility.

Management of Books of Business

Line underwriters are often expected to manage their book of business. Underwriting management usually passes down departmental goals to individual line underwriters. An insurer, for example, might want to limit the number of workers compensation policies it sells that are not accompanied by an account's other insurance. Likewise, line underwriters would be expected to help achieve that goal by writing workers compensation without supporting business *only* on a selective basis.

Some insurers also make line underwriters responsible for the book of business accepted from a producer. In these instances, not only should the line underwriter's book of business reflect insurer goals, but the books of business of each of the line underwriter's producers should as well.

Marketing Support

Insurer marketing efforts should coincide with the insurer's underwriting policy. Producers, for example, should not be encouraged to submit accounts that are clearly outside the insurer's underwriting guidelines. Likewise, line underwriters should not reject applications that meet insurer underwriting guidelines simply because of an underwriter's bias against a particular class of business.

Supporting the insurer's marketing objectives can also have broader implications for the line underwriter. Some insurers rely on **special agents** or **field representatives** to market the insurer and its products to agents and brokers. Some insurers have blended the responsibilities of special agents and line underwriters into the position of **production underwriter**. Production underwriters usually confer personally with producers and assist them with developing accounts that are acceptable to the insurer.

Underwriting Authority

Underwriting authority is the degree of decision-making latitude granted to underwriters. The underwriting authority granted to a line underwriter typically varies by position, grade level, and experience.

Underwriting authority requirements are usually communicated to an underwriter through the insurer's underwriting guide. A notation next to a specific classification in the underwriting guide, for example, might indicate that a senior underwriter must review and approve an application from that classification before it is processed further. Depending on the concerns that underwriting management places on a classification, underwriting approval might be required from the line underwriter's branch manager or a staff underwriter at the home office. Another approach to controlling underwriting authority is to specify in the underwriting guidelines the policy limits at which the accounts must be submitted to a higher authority.

Many insurers use information systems to manage underwriting authority. Rather than physically submit an account to others to review, insurer information systems are able provide those people who have approval responsibility with sufficient information to approve or disapprove the referred account. Information systems can also make it possible to identify those classifications that the insurer is making exceptions to write despite restrictions in the underwriting guidelines, and who is requesting them.

Some lines of insurance are so specialized that the insurers that write them prefer to centralize their line underwriters and, consequently, their underwriting authority. One insurer might, for example, have all applications for surety bonds, aviation accounts, and ocean marine submitted to line underwriters in the home office who are devoted to those specialties.

Some insurers extend underwriting authority to producers. These insurers find it to be more expeditious to empower their producers to exercise underwriting authority, as well as to pay claims, within a defined range. Normally, not all of an insurer's producers are granted underwriting authority, but those who are usually receive additional commission to compensate for the additional expenses incurred.

> ### "Front-Line" Underwriters
>
> The primary responsibility of a producer is to sell insurance. Many insurers, however, rely on their producers to "field underwrite" accounts. This means that the producer knows the types of accounts the insurer is interested in writing and submits those that are of the quality the insurer is usually willing to accept. Producers who can perform account selection before submitting the account to the insurer are often referred to as **front-line underwriters**. These producers save insurers from having to evaluate accounts that the insurer's underwriters will ultimately reject.

Even those producers who do not have underwriting authority know the types of accounts the insurer is actively seeking. Special agents or production underwriters, as well as periodic communication with the insurer, keep producers informed of the products the insurer wants to sell. Some insurers provide their producers with their underwriting guidelines so that issues regarding account acceptability can be determined before submission.

Establishing Underwriting Policy

As mentioned previously, an effective underwriting policy translates the goals of an insurer's senior management into rules and procedures that will guide individual and enterprise-wide underwriting decisions. Underwriting policy determines the composition of the insurer's book of business.

The composition of a book of business includes both the particular types of insurance products that the insurer will offer and the amount of business the insurer is willing to write, expressed in terms of limits of liability and policy count. It is common parlance in the insurance business to refer to insurance products as **lines of business**.

Lines of Business

The NAIC Annual Statement, which is prescribed for financial reporting in all states, divides property and liability coverages into thirty-eight separate lines of business. Examples of these statutory prescribed lines of business are fire, allied lines, workers compensation, commercial multiperil, and ocean marine. A complete listing appears in the NAIC Annual Statement. Insurers must report premiums, losses, and expenses by the lines of business, but related lines of business are combined to create insurance products. For example, an insurer who markets commercial auto insurance will have to offer the following NAIC Annual Statement lines of business: commercial auto no-fault (personal injury protection), other commercial auto liability, and commercial auto physical damage. When they use the term "line of business," underwriters are mentally combining several related NAIC Annual Statement lines into a single reference, such as "commercial auto."

Most insurers would like to expand premium writings, increase market share, and obtain profitable results. Establishing an underwriting policy, however, involves making compromises.

The principal dimensions of an insurer's underwriting policy are (1) the lines of business and classes to be written, (2) territories to be developed, and (3) forms, rates, and rating plans. The major constraining factors on underwriting policy are (1) capacity, (2) regulation, (3) personnel, and (4) reinsurance.

Once formulated, an insurer's underwriting policy must be implemented and monitored for effectiveness. A discussion of the logistics of putting an underwriting policy in place follows this discussion of factors that affect underwriting policy.

Capacity

An insurer's capacity refers to the relationship between premiums written and the size of policyholders' surplus, which is an insurer's net worth. That relationship is crucial in evaluating insurer solvency. The NAIC has developed a series of financial ratios that it uses in conjunction with analytical evaluations to identify insurers that should receive additional solvency surveillance from regulators. Premiums to surplus (net premiums written divided by policyholders' surplus) is one of those key ratios, and it is considered too high when it exceeds 300 percent, or 3-to-1.

Statutory Accounting Rules

Since the beginning of state oversight of insurance, insurance regulators have been primarily concerned with insurer solvency. The NAIC was formed in 1871 to reduce the inconsistencies and confusion caused by multiple state financial reporting requirements. The accounting system that evolved to satisfy insurance regulations is called **statutory accounting principles (SAP)**. SAP are conservative accounting rules designed to determine whether an insurer can meet its obligations to policyholders. Most other businesses use **generally accepted accounting principles (GAAP)**, which focus on the organization as an ongoing enterprise, for financial reporting.

One way for an insurer to exceed the premiums-to-surplus ratio is through the rapid growth of premiums written. Because of conservative accounting rules used in insurance, rapid growth results in a reduction in policyholders' surplus to pay for expenses generated by that growth. This constraint often precludes premium expansion unless the insurer purchases reinsurance or obtains more capital.

Insurers usually recognize the limitations of their capacity and seek to write those lines of business or accounts that maximize the insurer's return on equity. Insurers typically establish a return-on-equity threshold against which capacity allocation proposals are evaluated. If, for example, the insurer wants a 10 percent return on equity and the sale of workers compensation insurance in a specific state is expected to generate a 12 percent return on equity, then the insurer should expand into this territory and line of business if no better opportunity is present.

Regulation

States promulgate insurance regulations that are, to some extent, coordinated under the auspices of the NAIC. State regulation takes the form of statutes enacted by state legislatures and of regulations adopted by the state insurance department. Insurance regulation directly and indirectly affects most insurer activities.

Return on Equity

Return on equity is not only a benchmark for employing capacity but also a fundamental measure of insurer profitability. This financial ratio relates net operating gain (after taxes) as a percentage of prior-year capital and surplus.

The SAP and GAAP approaches to calculating return on equity differ, as shown below:

$$\frac{\text{Return on equity}}{\text{(SAP basis)}} = \frac{\text{Net income}}{\text{Average policyholders' surplus}}$$

$$\frac{\text{Return on equity}}{\text{(GAAP basis)}} = \frac{\text{Net income}}{\text{Average owners' equity}}$$

Stock insurers calculate both ratios since they report their financial performance using both SAP and GAAP bases. Mutual insurers calculate return on equity using only the SAP basis.

Return on equity is also a key financial ratio used by insurance regulators for solvency surveillance. An acceptable value for return on equity falls between 5 and 15 percent.

Regulation affects underwriting policy in several ways. Insurers must be licensed to write insurance in each state. Rates, rules, and forms must be filed with state regulators. Some states, such as Florida, specifically require underwriting guidelines to be filed. In addition to financial audits, state regulators perform market conduct examinations to ensure that insurers adhere to the classification and rating plans they have filed.

Insurance regulation is not applied equally among the states. In some jurisdictions, insurers might be unable to get rate filings approved, or approval might be granted so slowly that rate levels are inadequate relative to rising claim costs. Some insurers have chosen to withdraw from states that impose regulations they consider to be too restrictive.

Personnel

Insurers require the talents of specialists to market their products effectively, to underwrite specific lines of business, to service their accounts through loss control efforts, and to pay claims for losses that occur. An insurer must have a sufficient number of properly trained underwriters to implement its underwriting policy. No prudent insurer, for example, would pursue the highly technical lines of aviation, surety, or ocean marine insurance without a sufficient number of experienced underwriting specialists in those lines of business.

In addition to having the skilled personnel to perform the job, the insurer must have the personnel in place where they are needed. All things being equal, insurance theory suggests that premiums should be obtained from a broad range of insureds to create the widest possible distribution of loss exposures. As a practical matter, policyholder service requirements and expenses related to regulatory requirements do not permit financially limited insurers to engage in national operations. Insurers must have a sufficient volume of premium to operate efficiently in an area.

Reinsurance

The availability of adequate reinsurance and its cost are important considerations in developing underwriting policy. Reinsurance treaties might exclude certain lines or classes of business, or the cost of reinsurance might be prohibitive.

Reinsurers are also concerned with the underlying policy forms and coverages offered by the insurer. A reinsurer might not have any reservations concerning an insurer's use of forms developed by an insurance advisory organization but might expressly exclude reinsurance coverage for manuscript forms developed for a particular insured or forms developed independently of an insurance advisory organization.

Implementing Underwriting Policy

Underwriting management must communicate underwriting policy so it can be implemented. Most insurers convey underwriting policy through their underwriting guidelines, and underwriting audits are conducted to determine whether underwriting policy is being followed. Underwriting results gauge the effectiveness of underwriting policy.

Underwriting Guidelines

Because underwriting guidelines usually specify the attributes of accounts that insurers are willing to insure, insurers consider them to be trade secrets. Disclosure of this proprietary information might cause an insurer to lose its competitive advantage over others. The texts used in the Insurance Institute of America's Associate in Underwriting program do not advocate any particular underwriting policy or specify what should be contained in an insurer's underwriting guidelines. Rather, the program's aim is make the reader aware of the variety of successful approaches taken in the commercial insurance marketplace.

Some insurers have developed extensive underwriting guidelines with step-by-step instructions for handling particular classes of insureds. Such underwriting guidelines might identify specific hazards to evaluate, alternatives to consider, criteria to use in making the final decision, ways to implement the decision, and methods of monitoring the decision. The guidelines might also provide pricing instructions and information pertinent to the reinsurance program.

Some insurers take a less comprehensive approach to underwriting guidelines. For example, some underwriting guidelines might list all the commercial lines classifications and indicate their acceptability by line of business. One such approach is shown in Exhibit 1-1.

Underwriting guidelines serve the following purposes:

- They provide for structured decisions.
- They ensure uniformity and consistency.
- They synthesize insights and experience.
- They distinguish between routine and nonroutine decisions.
- They avoid duplication of effort.

Providing for Structured Decisions

Underwriting guidelines provide structure for underwriting decisions by identifying the major considerations underwriters should evaluate for each type of insurance written. The section of an insurer's underwriting guidelines addressing contractors' equipment, for example, might indicate that equipment *use* is of paramount importance in determining acceptability and pricing. Contractors' equipment used in mountainous areas is more likely subject to upset and overturn and therefore requires more scrutiny and premium than contractors' equipment used on flat terrain. By identifying the principal hazards associated with a particular class of business, underwriting guidelines ensure that underwriters consider the primary hazard traits of the exposures they evaluate.

Ensuring Uniformity and Consistency

Underwriting guidelines help ensure that selection decisions are made uniformly and consistently by all of the insurer's underwriters. Ideally, submissions that are identical in every respect should elicit the same underwriting response.

Exhibit 1-1
Commercial Underwriting Guidelines

I. GENERAL:

The Risk Selection Guide is a comprehensive alphabetical listing by class of business showing what the IIA Insurance Companies believe to be the desirability of insuring an average risk in the class. The Guide grades each class for Property, Commercial Automobile, Workers Compensation, Burglary and Robbery, Fidelity, Premises/Operations Liability, and Products/Completed Operations Liability. In addition, the final column titled "Form" indicates whether the General Liability coverage must be written on a Claims-Made Form (indicated by a "CM"), or whether the Occurrence Form is available (indicated by an "O"). Please remember the risk selection guide is only a guide. The company retains final authority regarding the acceptance or rejection of any specific risk.

II. CLASSIFICATION ACCEPTABILITY RATINGS:

The Risk Selection Guide is being published as a section of this agent's manual to answer the question: "Are risks within a particular class likely to be accepted by the IIA Insurance Companies"? In light of this question, the risk grades as found in the Risk Selection Guide are defined as follows:

E —Excellent

This class of business is considered to have excellent profit potential. Unless a specific risk in this class has unusual hazards or exposures, it will rarely present any underwriting problems. Risks graded as "E" may be bound by the agent without prior underwriting consent.

G —Good

This class of business is considered to have good profit potential. Normally this risk may be written before obtaining an inspection or developing additional underwriting information other than that present on the application. The agent may bind risks graded as "G" without prior underwriting consent.

A —Average

Potential for profit is marginal because of high variability of risks within the class. It is understood that the underwriter might think it is necessary to inspect the risk before authorizing binding. In all instances, it is recommended that the agent call the underwriter and discuss the risk before binding.

S —Submit

The account presents little potential for profit. These risks will require a complete written submission before binding. The underwriter *must* obtain a complete inspection and evaluate any other underwriting information deemed necessary before authorizing the binding of this risk.

D —Decline

Due to the lack of potential for profit, this class of risk is prohibited and will not be considered. Under no circumstances may a risk classified as "D" be bound without the prior written approval of the Vice President of Commercial Underwriting.

III. FOOTNOTES:

Footnotes sometimes are indicated as applying to an individual classification for a specific line of insurance. These footnotes are displayed at the bottom of each page and are designed to make you aware of certain hazards or exposures that are unacceptable or need to be addressed in an acceptable manner.

We hope the Risk Selection Guide will be valuable in understanding the types of business our companies want to be writing. However, please do not hesitate to call your underwriter if you are unsure as to how to classify a particular risk, or if you feel the factors associated with a specific risk make it considerably better or worse than the grading assigned by this guide.

Continued on next page.

Description	Form	Products & Completed Operations	Premises and Operations	Fidelity	Burglary and Robbery	Workers Compensation	Auto	Property
Painting—exterior—buildings or structures—three stories or less in height	O	G	G[2]	A	A	A	G	A[1]
Painting—interior—buildings or structures	O	G	G[2]	A	A	G	G	A[1]
Painting—oil or gasoline tanks	O	D	D	A	A	D	G	A[1]
Painting—ship hulls	O	D	D	A	A	D	G	A[1]
Painting—shop only	O	G	G	A	A	S	G	S[1,3]
Painting, picture, or frame stores	O	G	E	G	G	G	G	G
Paper coating or finishing	O	A	G	A	A	D	A	D
Paper corrugating or laminating—workers compensation only						D		
Paper crepeing—workers compensation only						D		
Paper goods manufacturing	O	G[4]	G[4]	A	A	D	A	D
Paper manufacturing	O	G[4]	G[4]	A	A	D	A	D
Paper products distributors	O	G[4]	G[4]	A	A	A	A	S
Paper, rag, or rubber stock dealers and distributors—secondhand	O	D	D	D	D	D	D	D
Paperhanging	O	G	G	G	G	G	G	G
Parachute manufacturing	O	D	D	D	D	D	A	D
Parades	O	A	A	S	S	S	A	A
Parking—private	O	A	A	S	S	S	A	A
Parking—public—open air	O	A	A	S	S	S	A	A
Parking—public—operated in conjunction with other enterprises	O	A	A	S	S	S	A	A
Parking—public—not open air	O	S	S	S	S	S	A	A
Parking—public shopping centers—(lessor's risk only)	O	G	G	G	G	S	G	G
Parks or playgrounds	O	S[5]	S[5]	A	A	A	A	A[5]
Paste, ink or mucilage manufacturing—workers compensation only						S		

1 Flammable liquid storage must be minimal and controlled.
2 A minimum property damage deductible of $250 on premises and operations coverage is mandatory.
3 The risk is unacceptable if any painting or finishing is done inside without an approved spray booth.
4 Acceptability will depend on the specific nature of the operation and specific types and uses of the products.
5 This risk is unacceptable unless this classification constitutes only a small part of other properties or operations.

Synthesizing Insights and Experience

Underwriting guidelines synthesize the insights and experience of seasoned underwriters. Staff underwriters, who assist with the insurer's unique or challenging accounts on a referral basis, often are able to include the approaches they have taken in underwriting particular classifications and lines of business. For many insurers, underwriting guidelines serve as a repository for an insurer's cumulative expertise.

Distinguishing Between Routine and Nonroutine Decisions

Underwriting guidelines help line underwriters to distinguish between routine and nonroutine decisions. Routine decisions are those for which the line underwriter clearly has decision-making authority according to the underwriting guidelines. Nonroutine decisions involve submissions that fall outside the authority granted the underwriter. Underwriting guides usually indicate that the classifications and lines of business must be either declined or submitted to a higher level of authority for approval.

Avoiding Duplication of Effort

Many underwriting situations recur. If the problems inherent in a particular situation have been identified and solved, the solution should apply to all similar situations that might arise in the future. Underwriting guidelines contain the information necessary to avoid costly duplication of effort.

Underwriting Audits

As mentioned, insurers use underwriting audits to determine whether underwriting decisions are being made in compliance with the insurer's underwriting guidelines. Additionally, underwriting audits provide valuable information on the effectiveness of the underwriting guidelines.

Underwriting guidelines cannot be allowed to stagnate if they are to serve the insurer in a dynamic insurance market. Underwriting audits help ensure that underwriting guidelines are responsive by identifying situations in which they are not followed because they are either outdated or considered to be unrealistic.

Staff underwriters also might discover that compliance with the insurer's underwriting guidelines is not having the result desired. As in those situations cited above, this information is valuable to the ongoing effort of developing useful underwriting guidelines.

Underwriting audits are typically conducted on-site at the branch or regional office being audited. Staff underwriters review individual accounts to determine whether underwriters have followed the underwriting guidelines and whether the underwriter has properly documented the file. Just as the underwriting audit provides the insurer with feedback on the effectiveness of the underwriting guidelines, the audit of individual files can provide individual line underwriters with strategies to improve future underwriting decisions.

Measuring Underwriting Results

Many insurers use the combined loss and expense ratio (or combined ratio) to measure the success of underwriting activities. The **combined ratio** is the sum of the insurer's loss ratio and expense ratio, as shown below.

$$\text{Combined ratio} = \text{Loss ratio} + \text{Expense ratio}$$

There are several ways to calculate the combined ratio.[9] The most commonly used approach is the **trade-basis combined ratio**, as shown below.

$$\frac{\text{Trade-basis}}{\text{combined ratio}} = \text{Loss ratio} + \text{Expense ratio}$$

$$\frac{\text{Trade-basis}}{\text{combined ratio}} = \frac{\text{Loss and loss adjustment expenses incurred}}{\text{Premiums earned}} + \frac{\text{Underwriting expenses incurred}}{\text{Premiums written}}$$

The denominators used in calculating the trade-basis combined ratio are different from each other. The loss ratio is calculated using premiums *earned*, while the expense ratio is calculated using premiums *written*. Insurance company analysts prefer this approach because it reflects insurance regulatory requirements on recognizing income and expenses.

Statutory accounting uses a conservative approach to recognizing income and expenses. Income is recognized only when earned, whereas expenses incurred are recognized immediately. Matching losses with *earned* premium rather than *written* premium is appropriate because insurer accounting rules require that an **unearned premium reserve** be established for coverage that has been paid for but not delivered. Pairing underwriting expenses incurred with *written* premium rather than *earned* premium recognizes that most underwriting expenses—primarily agents' commission and policy writing expenses—are incurred at the inception of each policy.

Although the combined ratio is the most often cited measure of underwriting success, the results that it produces are generally subject to an additional analysis of its components. How, for example, do the individual categories of insurer expenses compare to those of other insurers or to industry norms? What specific lines of business exceeded anticipated losses? An in-depth analysis permits an insurer to make attendant changes to its underwriting guidelines so desired results might be achieved in the future. Exhibit 1-2 shows the trade-basis combined ratio for all lines combined for the years 1989 through 1998. The insurance industry sustained an underwriting loss in all years of that period, with the combined ratio reaching its peak of 115.6 percent in 1992.

Changes in premium volume and delays in loss reporting can distort the results produced by the combined ratio. Additionally, any discussion of insurer underwriting profitability needs to be considered within the context of the underwriting cycle.

Changes in Premium Volume

Premium volume and underwriting policy are related. Restrictive underwriting policy usually means a reduced premium volume. Likewise, a less restrictive underwriting policy generally means an increased premium volume. Changes in underwriting policy, however, often do not have the immediate effect desired. An insurer, for example, that becomes more selective in its underwriting criteria will usually see a reduction in premiums written. Because incurred losses remain outstanding from the prior period that had a less restrictive underwriting policy, the loss ratio component of the combined ratio will likely deteriorate. With this reduction in premiums written, the expense ratio will increase, even though the insurer's underwriting expenses might have remained relatively unchanged. Likewise, a significant relaxation of underwriting standards, at least in the short term, can make an insurer appear profitable and even thrifty when its book of business is underpriced. As indicated, the combined ratio of an insurer must be evaluated, taking into consideration fluctuations in premium volume.

Delays in Loss Reporting

Delays in loss reporting reduce the value of the information provided by the combined ratio. If premiums and losses could be readily matched, an insurer could determine whether its book of business was underpriced and make corrections in its pricing structure. This information is of value to insurance regulators as well, because an inadequately priced book of business is a significant threat to an insurer's solvency.

Insurers establish a loss reserve amount when a claim is reported. Reserved losses are included in incurred losses and thereby reflected in the loss ratio. The type of loss usually determines how quickly the insurer is notified of a claim and how quickly the reserve is replaced with the amount of final

Exhibit 1-2

Property-Liability Insurance Trade-Basis Combined Ratio—All Lines Combined in the United States From 1989 to 1998

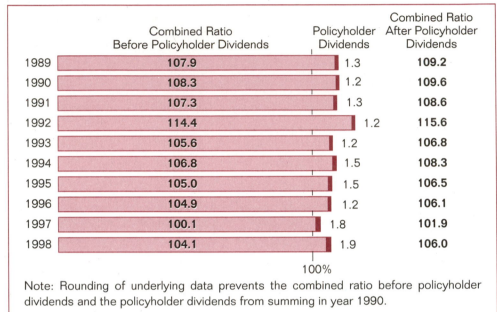

	Combined Ratio Before Policyholder Dividends	Policyholder Dividends	Combined Ratio After Policyholder Dividends
1989	107.9	1.3	109.2
1990	108.3	1.2	109.6
1991	107.3	1.3	108.6
1992	114.4	1.2	115.6
1993	105.6	1.2	106.8
1994	106.8	1.5	108.3
1995	105.0	1.5	106.5
1996	104.9	1.2	106.1
1997	100.1	1.8	101.9
1998	104.1	1.9	106.0

100%

Note: Rounding of underlying data prevents the combined ratio before policyholder dividends and the policyholder dividends from summing in year 1990.

Best's Aggregates & Averages—Property-Casualty, 1994 Edition, p. 63; 1999 Edition, p. 103.

payment. A claim arising from a fender bender is a good example of a claim that will likely be settled quickly. Although property and some liability claims are settled in days and weeks, many liability claims can take years to be completely resolved. An obstetrician, for example, may injure a child during the baby's delivery. The injury itself may not be manifest for some time, so that the parents are unaware that negligence has occurred. Regardless of any legal settlement reached between the physician and the parents, the child can bring suit when he or she reaches majority (usually age eighteen). The physician's medical malpractice insurer, in this instance, will not be able to completely determine the ultimate value of this claim for years. Claims that have a long loss development (often referred to as "long-tail" claims) can cause an insurer's loss ratio to be understated and the book of business to be underpriced.

In addition to individual loss reserves for known losses, insurers establish reserves for **incurred-but-not-reported (IBNR)** losses. IBNR losses have several components: reserves for increases in reported losses, reserves for reopened claims, reserves for reported but not recorded losses, and gross IBNR losses. **Gross IBNR** is a reserve amount that reflects the insurer's best estimate of losses that have occurred but that it may not find out about for several years.

Accurately estimating gross IBNR is one of the challenges insurers must address. As mentioned, a low gross IBNR could mean an underpriced book of business. A high gross IBNR could make the insurer appear unprofitable even when it is not. A mistake in reserving will also be reflected in the pricing of future policies.

Underwriting Cycle

Historically, insurance industry underwriting results have been cyclical: a period of underwriting profits has been followed by a period of underwriting losses. When insurers earn underwriting profits, they decrease their rates and offer broader coverage to expand market share. At times when underwriting losses prevail, insurers increase rates and restrict the availability of coverage. Insurers refer to this change in the market state as the **underwriting cycle**.

For a long time, the underwriting cycle was fairly consistent and predictable, repeating itself about every six years. In the early 1970s, however, the cycle began to lengthen. Periods of underwriting profits remained about the same, but periods of underwriting losses became longer. The cycle also became more volatile. Combined ratios in the peak of the cycle (when underwriters were sustaining losses) became higher. In response to heavier losses, underwriters became more selective and their rate increases became more pronounced. These market swings produced insurance availability crises. The peaks and troughs of the underwriting cycle are shown in Exhibit 1-3.

Exhibit 1-3
Phases of the Underwriting Cycle

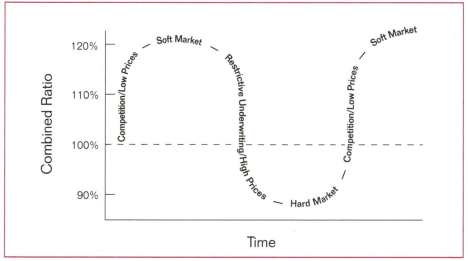

For the past decade, the insurance industry has been in what appears to be an extended **soft market** in which insurers have cut prices and have offered broader coverages. Insurance industry analysts expected the substantial losses insurers sustained because of Hurricane Hugo in 1989 to cause the cycle to return to a **hard market** in which insurance prices rise (and profits along with them), but this did not happen. Even the multiple catastrophes of 1992 did not have a widespread effect on rate levels or combined ratios.[10] Although rates increased in Florida and other affected coastal areas following Hurricane Andrew, for example, the overall insurance market continued to reduce prices.

Economists who have studied the continued soft market in property and liability insurance have concluded that overall insurer profits—underwriting results tempered by investment results—have been a significant force affecting pricing in the insurance marketplace.[11] Perhaps, then, the traditional focus on the underwriting cycle should shift to the cyclical activity of combined net income, which is often measured by the operating profit ratio.

The **operating profit** (or **loss**) **ratio** is the sum of underwriting profit or loss (combined ratio) and investment profit or loss (net investment ratio). As Exhibit 1-4 shows, investment earnings have offset underwriting losses for the insurance industry as a whole.

Standards of Performance

One nonfinancial technique that can be used to evaluate the performance of an underwriting department is to set standards, or measures, of performance regarding several crucial areas of underwriting. These underwriting performance standards include the following areas of underwriting:

- Selection
- Product or line of business mix
- Pricing
- Accommodated accounts
- Retention ratio
- Success ratio
- Service to producers
- Premium to underwriter

The line of business written and the goals of underwriting management determine which of these performance standards is more important.

Exhibit 1-4

Property-Liability Insurance Operating Profit or Loss—All Lines Combined in the United States From 1989 to 1998

	Underwriting Profit or Loss (Combined Ratio)*	Net Investment Ratio	Operating Ratio
1989	109.0	15.0	94.0
1990	109.4	15.2	94.2
1991	108.7	15.3	93.4
1992	115.6	14.8	100.8
1993	106.9	13.9	93.0
1994	108.3	13.9	94.3
1995	106.5	14.5	92.0
1996	106.1	14.6	91.4
1997	101.9	15.5	86.4
1998	106.0	14.6	91.4

100%

*After policyholder dividends

Note: Rounding of underlying data prevents the combined ratio after policyholder dividends less the net investment ratio from equaling operating ratio in years 1994 and 1996.

Best's Aggregates & Averages—Property-Casualty, 1994 Edition, p. 63; 1999 Edition, p. 103.

Selection

Insurers often establish selection goals for underwriters in order to ensure that the *quality* of the underwriter's book of business does not deteriorate. For example, an underwriter might be required to have specific percentages of its book of business be considered "highly desirable," "average," and "below average." For this type of performance standard to be effective, the insurer's underwriting guidelines need to clearly delineate between account categories. Selection standards for individual underwriters usually support overall underwriting goals and are evaluated during an underwriting audit.

Product or Line of Business Mix

This performance measure requires a statement in the insurer's underwriting guidelines of the desired product mix for new and renewal business. For example, if product liability losses are causing an adverse effect on the insurer's entire book of business, the product mix standard might require a reduction in manufacturing classes and a concerted effort to increase the writing in the contractor, service, and mercantile classes. The comparison of the actual book to the desired one provides a straightforward evaluation of performance.

Pricing

Insurers usually track the extent to which their underwriters deviate from the insurer's established pricing for specific classifications. Insurer underwriting information systems are often used to monitor an underwriter's book of business. This information might be useful in determining to what extent the underwriter's book of business is underpriced or overpriced and where pricing adjustments might be made, should market conditions change.

Accommodated Accounts

Making an underwriting accommodation usually means accepting substandard exposures in return for other, more profitable accounts. This performance standard evaluates whether the underwriter is making excessive accommodations and whether the agent or broker is actually submitting the superior accounts as promised. Many underwriters maintain an accommodation log in which all accommodated accounts are entered, along with the reasons for the deviation from the insurer's underwriting guidelines.

Retention Ratio

The retention ratio is the percentage of expiring policies that an insurer renews. Retention can be measured by policy count, premium volume, or both. Since most, if not all, of the underwriting investigation work has been performed for existing policies, keeping those policies offers more profit potential than acquiring new business does. A low retention rate might indicate serious deficiencies in the way insurers do business, including poor service to producers, noncompetitive pricing, or unfavorable claims service. This standard of performance requires careful monitoring of the renewal rate and evaluation of any trends discerned.

Success Ratio

The success ratio is the ratio of new business written to new business quoted. Underwriting management usually monitors this performance measure more closely than the other standards of performance because the success ratio provides information about the insurer's competitiveness in the current insurance market. A success ratio that is inordinately either high or low might require further investigation. A high success ratio might indicate any of the following market conditions:

- Easing of competition
- Rate inadequacy or rates lower than other insurers'
- Broader coverage than other insurers'
- Deterioration in selection criteria
- An extremely good relationship between the insurer and the agent or broker

Alternatively, a low success ratio might indicate one or more of the following market conditions:

- Increasing competition
- Rates that are too high
- Coverages or forms that are too restrictive
- Selection criteria that are too stringent
- Poor service
- A poor relationship between the insurer and the agent or broker

Service to Producers

Producers work most frequently with insurers who work most cooperatively with them. Because producers usually rank insurers on the basis of service received, the insurer must be able to evaluate its own performance. This standard requires establishing a set of minimum acceptable standards for certain types of service to producers. The actual performance of each underwriter, branch, or region being evaluated is then compared with the mandated level of performance. An example of one such standard appears in Exhibit 1-5.

Exhibit 1-5
Example of "Service to Producers" Underwriting Standard

	Category	Minimum Acceptable Standard
1.	Quotations	3 working days
2.	New policies	3 working days
3.	Replies to correspondence	2 working days
4.	Cancellations, endorsements, certificates	5 working days
5.	Direct cancellation notices	Same-day service
6.	Renewals	No later than 10 days before expiration

Premium to Underwriter

The volume of premium an underwriter is able to handle is an often-used measure of performance. Underwriting management uses this measure to determine whether individual underwriters are doing their share of work.

The Underwriting Process

Underwriters need to be good decision makers. Underwriting is not an easy task; therefore, becoming good at it requires time. As an underwriter gains experience, making underwriting decisions becomes increasingly routine. Complex accounts challenge even the experienced underwriter. Until an underwriter has sufficient experience to handle most accounts confidently, it is helpful to follow a specific process as a guide to decision making.

The underwriting process can be described as consisting of these five steps:

1. Gathering information
2. Identifying, developing, and evaluating alternatives
3. Selecting an alternative
4. Implementing the decision
5. Monitoring the account

This section will describe each of those steps.

The Myth of Underwriting Intuition

Underwriters have traditionally been reluctant to admit that their "underwriting intuition" is actually an internalized decision-making process that can apply to a variety of loss exposures. A valid justification for this reluctance is that underwriters recognize the difficulty of defining one process that encapsulates their thought process. Perhaps the skill described as underwriting intuition would better be described as the creative application of the underwriting process.

Gathering Information

Having information about an account is vital to making a good underwriting decision. Underwriters obtain most of the information they need from the insurance application. Often, the information presented there is either insufficient or it raises concerns that cause the underwriter to seek this information. Underwriters may seek this information from several sources so that they can make a decision.

Gathering information about an account must be done judiciously because of the costs involved. Underwriters must consider whether the information they want is appropriate to the account they are evaluating. For example, does an application for a restaurant justify a study of the food service industry? What effect, if any, will any lack of information have on the decision? The balance that underwriters must maintain between the hazards presented by the account and the information needed to underwrite it is often referred to as **information efficiency**. The use of underwriting information is the focus of Chapter 3 of this text.

Hazard Evaluation

A **hazard** is any condition that increases the expected frequency or severity of loss. Hazards can result from any number of sources and are usually classified as physical, moral, and morale. Much underwriting information is developed to enable the underwriter to identify and evaluate hazards. Underwriters want to know whether the hazards associated with a particular account are typical of similarly classified accounts.

Physical Hazards

Physical hazards are tangible characteristics of the property, persons, or operations to be insured that affect the expected frequency and severity of loss from one or more causes of loss. Physical hazards can be attributes of the applicant, of the property to be insured, or of the environment in which the property is located. An untrained driver, susceptibility to damage of cargo being shipped, and poor housekeeping practices are all examples of physical hazards.

Moral Hazards

A **moral hazard** is a condition that exists when a policyholder tries to cause a loss or exaggerates a loss that has occurred. Although most information on moral hazard is subjective, objective data might be available, such as a history of past financial difficulties, criminal records, or other public records. Unacceptable conduct, once made public, often makes news in local papers. Agents and brokers usually have that local contact and can pass along this information to the underwriter. Potential indicators of moral hazard include weak financial condition, undesirable associates, and poor moral character.

Weak Financial Condition   The owners of a financially weak commercial enterprise might intentionally cause a loss in order to obtain desperately needed cash. For example, the Persian Gulf War of 1991 and fear of domestic terrorism presented a backdrop for an insurance fraud attempt. The owners of two million gallons of sodium hydrosulfate stored near the Norfolk Naval Base in Virginia planted pipe bombs at their facility after doubling their property insurance. Had the owners been successful in their fraudulent claim, they would have been able to eliminate their back debts and make a $1 million profit.[12] Ocean marine underwriters are particularly aware that, during periods of excess capacity in the marketplace, the owners of an idle or obsolete vessel might try to "sell it to the underwriters" by intentionally causing a loss.

Since the financial condition of a business can change quickly, detecting the hazard caused by weak financial condition requires frequent monitoring. Changes in consumer tastes or innovation by competitors can leave a business with a sizable obsolete inventory. The insured's financial difficulties can postpone essential maintenance to vital services such as electrical, plumbing, and heating systems.

Undesirable Associates   A policyholder's association with criminals is another indicator of potential moral hazard. A business that is frequented by members of the underworld or other undesirables does not reflect well on the character of the proprietor.

Poor Moral Character   Moral hazard can arise from the poor moral character of the policyholder even when the financial condition is sound. Previous questionable losses, a criminal record, or evidence of moral turpitude can indicate a moral hazard. A reputation for unethical or illegal business practices would also indicate moral hazard.

Morale Hazards

Morale hazard is a condition that exists when people are less careful than they should be because of the existence of insurance. That hazard arises out of carelessness or indifference to loss and is usually more subtle and more difficult to detect than moral hazard. Morale hazard might better be termed the "lack of motivation hazard" because it exists in policyholders who are poorly motivated to avoid and minimize losses. Morale hazards might be indicated by poor personality, poor management, or weak financial condition.

Poor or inefficient management can also indicate morale hazard. Sloppy housekeeping and indifferent bookkeeping are overt manifestations of this condition. Indifference to loss can result in the neglect of maintenance of fire extinguishers and other safety devices. Poor or nonexistent internal control systems invite theft and embezzlement by employees. Failure to comply with recommendations or to cooperate with loss control personnel is a further indication of morale hazard.

Identifying, Developing, and Evaluating Alternatives

After all the essential information on a particular submission has been gathered and exposures have been evaluated, the underwriter is ready to make a decision. The underwriter must identify and develop the alternatives available regarding the submission and, after carefully evaluating each alternative, choose the optimal one under the circumstances.

Two alternatives are easily identified: the underwriter can accept the submission as is or reject it. Additionally, the underwriter can accept the submission *subject* to certain modifications. Determining the modification that best meets the needs of the insurer, producer, and applicant can be a challenge.

Typical modifications that can be made are as follows:

- Adopting loss control programs or devices
- Changing rates, rating plans, or policy limits
- Amending policy terms and conditions
- Using facultative reinsurance

Selecting an Alternative

Selecting an alternative involves weighing the positive and negative features of a submission. The underwriter must identify and evaluate the exposures, assess the degree of risk relative to the average exposure contemplated in the rate, review the controls and protection features in place, and assess management's commitment to loss prevention. Additional factors that need to be considered before the underwriter makes a decision are as follows:

- The amount of underwriting authority required
- The presence of supporting business
- The mix of business
- Producer relationships
- Regulatory constraints

Amount of Underwriting Authority Required

Before accepting an applicant, an underwriter must determine whether he or she has the necessary underwriting authority to make the decision. The underwriter's task differs according to whether he or she has sufficient authority to decide or whether he or she must prepare the file for submission to a higher underwriting authority. The underwriter should check the underwriting guidelines before promising a producer a quick answer on a submission, since referral to higher underwriting authority can be time-consuming.

Presence of Supporting Business

Insurers usually discourage underwriters from writing one line of business for an insured without supporting lines of business. Often, another insurer has accepted the desirable lines of business but is unwilling to offer a particular coverage or is unwilling to offer needed coverage at an affordable price. Some underwriters seize this opportunity to write some of the insured's coverage with the expectation that they will have a chance to quote the balance of the account at renewal.

Generally, underwriters prefer to practice **account underwriting**, whereby all of the business from a particular applicant is evaluated as a whole. Underwriters are much more likely to accept marginal lines of business from an insured if the account appears profitable overall.

Mix of Business

The **mix of business** is the distribution of individual policies that compose the book of business of a producer, territory, state, or region among the various lines and classifications. Underwriting policy, as determined by management and as specified in the underwriting guidelines, will frequently indicate the insurer's goals regarding the mix of business. Particular classifications, such as contractors in general liability insurance or restaurants in property coverage, might represent too large a share of the present book of business. To restore balance, the insurer might decide to raise the criteria for acceptance or to prohibit new business entirely.

Producer/Insurer Relationships

The relationship between the insurer and the producer should be based on mutual trust and respect. Differences of opinion are common, particularly since some of the goals of producers conflict with those of the underwriters. Nevertheless, the long-run goals of both producers and insurers are growth and profit. Mutual accommodation and willingness to see the other's point of view are essential to building a satisfactory working relationship.

Regulatory Constraints

Insurance regulations in most states place restrictions on an insurer's ability to cancel or nonrenew an insurance policy. These restrictions are usually codified within the state's unfair trade practices laws. After a policy takes effect, insurers often have a free-look period during which they can investigate an account and for which there are few restrictions on canceling coverage. Underwriters must make timely underwriting decisions to avoid mandatory acceptance or renewal of an otherwise unacceptable account.

Implementing the Decision

Implementing underwriting decisions generally involves three steps. The first step is communicating the decision to the producer and to other insurer personnel. If the decision is to accept the account with modifications, the modifications and the reasons must be clearly communicated to the producer or applicant, and the applicant must agree to the modifications. The insurer must establish procedures to verify that modifications requested are implemented, particularly loss control recommendations. If the underwriter decides to reject the application, he or she should try to communicate this decision to the producer in a positive way to avoid damaging their long-term relationship. Underwriters must present clear and logical reasons for why the particular applicant does not meet the insurer's underwriting criteria. Effective communication of both positive and negative decisions clarifies the insurer's standards as market conditions change.

The second step is developing appropriate documentation. Underwriters often rely on underwriting technicians to issue a binder or to have the policy issued. In some lines of business, the underwriter might ask underwriting technicians to prepare certificates of insurance and file the certificates with appropriate authorities, such as the United States Department of Transportation for motor carrier accounts.

Binders

Most insurance clients need coverage to take effect immediately. Insurers authorize producers to "bind coverage," pending underwriting acceptance or rejection of the account. Written evidence of temporary coverage is called a **binder**. A binder can be oral, with coverage requested over the phone, but usually oral binders are reduced to writing. All policy provisions are effective the moment the binder is issued. The binder is effective either until the insured receives actual notice of cancellation or until the policy is issued. The binder should specify types of coverages and coverage limits desired. Because insurers are responsible for losses on bound policies before an underwriting evaluation can occur, underwriters are usually asked to identify situations in which producers abuse their binding authority.

The third step is to record information about the policy and the applicant for accounting, statistical, and monitoring purposes. Data entry personnel extract essential information, so information systems will contain details on each policy written. For example, the premium must be posted in order to bill the producer. Data about the policyholder includes location, limits, coverages, price modifications, class, and risk features. That data must be captured so that the insurer and the industry can accumulate information on all accounts for ratemaking, statutory reporting, financial accounting, and book of business evaluations.

Monitoring the Account

Accounts must be monitored to ensure that they remain acceptable to the insurer. Underwriters can expect that accounts will change over time. An insured might add a new location, purchase another business, or enter into another area of operation. Although insurance-related consequences are likely a minor aspect of these business decisions, underwriters are interested in changes that could affect the likelihood of loss.

Account monitoring can begin immediately after the policy is written. Claim activity, coverage change requests, and other policy activity are events that usually cause an underwriter to monitor an account. For example, a sizable loss might trigger the insurer's information system to notify the underwriter. The underwriter can then review the claim information to determine whether the loss that occurred is consistent with the types of losses expected. Most underwriters will follow up with the producer on large losses, losses from previously unidentified operations, and frequent losses. Similar underwriting monitoring activity might be initiated from loss control reports or premium audit reports.

Summary

Underwriting is the process of selecting policyholders through hazard recognition and evaluation, pricing, and determination of policy terms and conditions. The practice of underwriting insurance policies began when insurance emerged as a commercial enterprise. In modern practice, underwriters strive to develop a large market share of profitable business. Adverse selection, a natural opponent of this objective, occurs when the applicant for insurance presents a higher-than-average probability of loss than is expected from a truly random sample of all applicants. Underwriting activities are typically described with a distinction between day-to-day risk selection activities (line functions) and management activities (staff functions).

Establishing underwriting policy is a key objective of senior management. Effectively implementing underwriting policy is a criterion for the success of any insurer. An insurer's underwriting policy promotes the type and classes of insurance anticipated to produce a growing and profitable book of business. Although almost any restriction on acceptable business can be imposed, there are limitations on what an underwriting policy can contain and limiting factors to that underwriting policy.

Implementing underwriting policy means communicating which lines of business and classifications are desirable to line underwriters. Insurers use a written manual or underwriting guidelines as the primary tool for disseminating underwriting policy. Staff underwriters perform underwriting audits to determine whether line underwriters are following the insurer's underwriting guidelines.

Most insurers use the trade-basis combined ratio to measure underwriting success. A combined ratio of less than 100 percent means that the insurer had profitable underwriting results, whereas a combined ratio of greater than 100 percent indicates an underwriting loss. The combined ratio ignores investment income, which has been an important component of insurer's overall profitability and financial stability for the past several decades. There are other, nonfinancial measures of individual underwriter performance, such as selection and pricing standards.

The underwriting process can be viewed as a five-step decision-making process:

1. Gathering information
2. Identifying, developing, and evaluating alternatives
3. Selecting an alternative
4. Implementing the decision
5. Monitoring the account

This chapter discussed each of those steps in a manner that can be applied to any specific line of business or insurance product.

Chapter Notes

1. Robert J. Gibbons, George E. Rejda, and Michael W. Elliott, *Insurance Perspectives* (Malvern, PA: American Institute for Chartered Property Casualty Underwriters, 1992), pp. 7-8.
2. Barry D. Smith and Eric A. Wiening, *How Insurance Works* (Malvern, PA: Insurance Institute of America, 1994), p. 3.

3. Joseph F. Mangan and Connor M. Harrison, *Advanced Underwriting Techniques* (Malvern, PA: The Insurance Institute of America, 1995). *Advanced Underwriting Techniques* is a text assigned in the Insurance Institute of America's AU 66 course, Commercial Underwriting: Liability and Advanced Techniques.

4. Home page for Insurance Services Office, World Wide Web: http//www.iso.com

5. Home page for National Council Compensation Insurance, World Wide Web: http//www.2.ncci.com

6. Home page for American Association of Insurance Services, World Wide Web: http//www.aais.org

7. Mangan and Harrison, *Underwriting Commercial Property* (Malvern, PA: Insurance Institute of America, 1995). *Underwriting Commercial Property* is a text assigned in the Insurance Institute of America's AU 65 course, Commercial Underwriting: Principles and Property.

8. Mangan and Harrison, *Underwriting Commercial Liability*, 2nd ed. (Malvern, PA: Insurance Institute of America, 2000). *Underwriting Commercial Liability* is a text assigned in the Insurance Institute of America's AU 66 course, see no. 3, *supra.*

9. The financial basis combined ratio is another way of calculating the combined ratio. The difference between the financial and trade calculations is the use of premium earned in the denominator of the expense ratio.

10. Losses from hurricanes Andrew and Iniki and the Los Angeles riots made 1992 the worst year on record for catastrophe losses. *Fact Book 2000* (New York: Insurance Information Institute, 2000), p. 3.4

11. Barbara D. Stewart, *The Profit Cycle in Property and Casualty Insurance* (Malvern, PA: American Institute for Chartered Property Casualty Underwriters, 1997).

12. "Three Arrested in Fraud Scheme," *Business Insurance*, February 18, 1991, p. 11.

Chapter 2

Underwriting the Commercial Organization

Successful risk selection requires that underwriters know what an account's loss exposures are so they can be evaluated. Such knowledge is obtained, in part, on an account-by-account basis as the specific activities and operations of the insured are analyzed. The underwriting approach described in the texts used for the Associate in Underwriting program suggests that individual accounts must be evaluated relative to the "average" account that was contemplated in the insurer's pricing. This approach to risk selection assumes that the underwriter has a thorough understanding of the prospective insured, in addition to the range of accounts that are included in the prospective insured's classification.

Underwriters need to know the basics of business so that they can evaluate the operation and conduct of an account submitted for insurance. The insured's form of ownership provides underwriters an indication of the extent of the insured's operations and organizational limitations that might affect the account's underwriting desirability. Businesses rely on the work of others: employees and independent contractors. Underwriters usually want to know the control the account exercises over its operations. Underwriters need to know what businesses do in a broad sense. Underwriting tools described in Chapter 3 provide information on many specific types of businesses. This chapter provides an approach to learning about an industry sector and the insured's place in it.

Types of Business Ownership

Underwriters need to understand the fundamentals of business ownership so they will know who is being insured, to what extent the coverage provided is meeting the needs of the insured, and how the insured should be named in the policy.

While there are many types of business ownership, the most common types of business ownership are as follows:

- Sole proprietorships
- Partnerships
- Corporations

An account's form of ownership is indicative of its management structure. A key, but often elusive, underwriting attribute of a commercial account is the quality of the insured's management. As described in the sections that follow, an account's form of ownership often affects the demands placed on its management. An insured that is experiencing rapid expansion, for example, might not have the management resources needed to properly direct its growth. For these accounts, insurance-related issues such as housekeeping and property maintenance might be of minimal concern. Additionally, an account's form of ownership can help or hinder its financial stability, as well as affect its access to financial resources.

Sole Proprietorships

Sole proprietorships are unincorporated businesses owned by *one* person. Sole proprietorships include large enterprises with many employees and hired managers, as well as part-time operations in which the owner is the only person involved. Sole proprietorships account for about 70 percent of all business entities in the United States.[1]

Advantages of Sole Proprietorships

Ease of formation and limited capital requirements are two of the primary reasons for the popularity of sole proprietorships. Sole proprietorships are usually subject to minimal state and federal control other than obtaining required state and local licenses and permits. Sole proprietorship profits are included in the owner's personal income and not taxed separately. While some businesses need more financial resources to start and operate than other businesses, most sole proprietors begin operation with a limited investment.

Perhaps the most compelling reason that people want to form sole proprietorships is their desire to be their own boss and work for themselves. A sole proprietor has full control of the business and is fully responsible for its operation. Pride in ownership—a trait important in underwriting—means the willingness of the business owner to work hard to make the business succeed.

Disadvantages of Sole Proprietorships

Unlimited liability is the most significant disadvantage of a sole proprietorship. **Unlimited liability** means that if the business becomes bankrupt, creditors can seize business and even personal assets to satisfy claims. Potentially, the owner may lose not only his or her business, but his or her home and other property as well. Sole proprietorships are often thinly financed and remain so because of difficulty in obtaining needed funds.

Pressure on the sole proprietor that stems from running the business can sometimes be insurmountable. Sole proprietors often go into business for themselves because they have a special skill, a specific expertise, or a unique knowledge that they can offer to others. As a business grows, the role of the owner often must change. The owner-artisan, for example, might have to hire others to create products or provide services while the owner addresses the managerial aspects of the business. Sometimes, the burden of operating a business—keeping high-quality employees, meeting payrolls, obtaining funds to pay creditors, and satisfying customers—becomes too much for one person to comfortably manage. Some sole proprietorships fail because this form of business ownership does not offer the owner sufficient flexibility as the demands of business grow and change.

Business Risks

Sole proprietorships often have business risks that require the owner's attention much more than its pure loss exposures do. Because business assets are essential to the sole proprietorship and not easily replaced, a comprehensive risk management program, generally grounded in insurance, is essential.

Business risks are those assumed by an enterprise as part of its operation. Failure to get approval from the FDA for a new drug, for example, would be a business risk for a pharmaceutical company. Business risks generally occupy the attention of the business's management. Insurance texts often categorize business risks as **speculative risks**, for which there is a chance of a gain as well as a loss. Insurance underwriters are chiefly concerned with **pure risks**, for which there is a chance only of loss. Examples of pure risks are losses caused by fire, theft, and windstorm.

Partnerships

Partnerships are unincorporated businesses of two or more persons, each of which has a financial interest in the business. The "persons" in a partnership could be individuals, estates, trusts, other partnerships, or corporations. Partners are jointly liable for the debts of the business. Unlike a sole proprietorship, a partnership is recognized as an entity distinct from its individual members for certain purposes. A partnership, for example, can sue and be sued, as well as own and convey real estate. Partnerships, like sole proprietorships, do not pay taxes. Partnership profits are passed to partners, who pay taxes on the business's earnings.

There are two types of partnerships: general and limited. **General partnerships** are a form of partnership in which *each* partner usually has an active role in the business and assumes unlimited liability. **Limited partnerships**, in contrast, enable their limited partners to avoid having unlimited liability. Limited partnerships have at least one general partner who must assume unlimited liability for all business debts. Limited partners are able to invest in the partnership but are forbidden by law to participate in its active management.

General and limited partners can be secret, silent, dormant, or nominal. **Secret partners** are general partners who are active in the business but who are not known to the public. **Silent partners** are known to the public but not active in the business. **Dormant partners** are neither known by the public nor active in the business. Partners who want to limit their involvement in a partnership to that of being an investor often choose to be dormant and limited partners. **Nominal partners** are usually not true partners because they have no investment in the partnership. Nominal partners often lend their expertise or experience to the partnership and might even represent themselves as a partner in the business when really they are not.

The **articles of partnership** is a legal document that specifies each partner's financial and managerial responsibilities toward one another. This partnership agreement includes all types of partners and usually specifies the following:

- Each partner's name
- The investment of each partner
- Each partner's share of profits
- The duties of each partner
- The salary, if any, of each partner
- A method of withdrawing from the partnership
- A method of dissolving the partnership

The partners usually divide earnings and losses equally among themselves. Sometimes, the partnership agreement provides a greater share of profits for partners who make a greater contribution to the partnership. Some partners may be paid a salary in addition to their share of the profits. The partnership must reimburse each partner for any payments made and any personal liability incurred in the course of the firm's business.

Unless the partnership agreement states otherwise, each partner has an equal voice in the management of the partnership. The partnership agreement could, for instance, place the management responsibility with one of the partners or with a nonpartner. Usually, all partners participate in the management of the business.

Dissolution of a partnership occurs at the death of any partner. The heirs of the deceased partner are entitled to their respective shares of the business. The remaining partners can choose to form a new partnership, but the original partnership arrangement is terminated. To counteract the limited and uncertain longevity of partnerships, many partnerships purchase life insurance on each partner to pay heirs and avoid the need to liquidate assets as part of a formal plan to continue the business.

When a partnership is dissolved—and it can be dissolved for reasons other than the death of a partner—a partner's right to act on behalf of the partnership ends, except to do what may be necessary to conclude the partnership's business affairs. Dissolution includes converting partnership assets to cash to pay creditors and distributing the remainder to the partners.

Advantages of Partnerships

In addition to favorable tax treatment, partnerships generally have greater access to capital through the combined wealth of the partners. Each partner also often brings needed talents to the partnership. Partnership management responsibilities can be spread among the partners. As with sole proprietorships, partnerships are easy to establish and have few governmental restrictions on their formation.

Disadvantages of Partnerships

Individual partners have unlimited liability for the debts of the partnership, so wealthy partners are potentially subject to a higher contribution than the other partners in order to satisfy creditor claims. Limited partners, described above, are an exception to unlimited partnership obligations in that their liability is limited to their investment in the partnership. Partnerships have a limited existence because many events—notably the death of a partner—can cause partnership dissolution. The illiquid financial investment of partners into the partnership can only be recovered by dissolution or finding a willing buyer, which is usually the other partners. Shared partnership management—an advantage in many respects—can also lead to conflict among the partners. Like sole proprietorships, partnership financial resources are limited to the personal wealth of the owners and to amounts that can be borrowed.

Corporations

Corporations are artificial beings, invisible, intangible, and existing only in the contemplation of the law. Corporations can be public or private. **Public corporations** are owned by the general public. Public corporations' stock is usually sold on stock exchanges such as the New York Stock Exchange (NYSE) and the National Association of Securities Dealers Automated Quotation System (NASDAQ). **Private corporations** are owned by only a few stockholders, and ownership of their stock is usually not open to the public. Many private corporations are family owned, and control of the stock—and thereby control of the corporation—is commonly described as being "closely held." Corporations have unique features that make them highly suited to meet the needs of businesses.

Corporations are controlled by a **board of directors**. The corporation's board hires the management to operate the business. Stockholders, the owners of a corporation, are entitled to one vote for each share of stock owned. Stockholders elect the board of directors. Additionally, stockholders may be asked to vote on changes to the corporate charter, mergers, changes in general policies, or other matters proposed for stockholder consent.

Directors of corporations have responsibilities to the corporation and the stockholders. Directors have a legal duty to be loyal to the corporation and the stockholders and to act in their best interests. This obligation means that a director must avoid conflicts of interest and not use his or her position for personal gain. Directors must use proper business judgment and avoid gross negligence. Corporate directors can make mistakes, but they are expected to make informed, reasoned decisions that demonstrate a duty of care even if the results the decision produces are unfavorable or unexpected. Directors are expected to comply with securities laws. The Securities Acts of 1933 and 1934 created corporate-director obligations to provide complete and reliable financial information about the corporation's securities. When society challenges the operation of a corporation, the board of directors is often required to respond.

Advantages of Corporations

Corporations are considered to be entities legally separate from their owners. Stockholders have limited liability for corporation debts. Stockholders may lose the value of their investment in the corporation, but they will not be required to surrender personal assets to pay corporate debts.

Most corporate charters grant an unlimited life to corporations. Corporations, therefore, are perpetual organizations that exist independently of their owners, unlike sole proprietorships and partnerships.

Corporate ownership can be acquired and transferred easily. Public corporations usually have thousands of stockholders, and active markets enable people to buy and sell their interests in corporations. Unlike the other forms of business ownership, corporations enable stockholders to have a fairly liquid investment.

Corporations regularly employ specialists and hire consultants to perform tasks. In contrast, sole proprietorships and partnerships often have limited managerial depth and may not have the financial resources to access needed skills.

Perhaps the most important attribute of a corporation is its ability to raise capital. Corporations sell stock and issue bonds to raise funds. Additionally, corporations often have significant assets that can be used as collateral when borrowing money from lending institutions. Expansion plans for sole proprietorships and partnerships are limited to the personal financial resources of their owners.

Disadvantages of Corporations

Corporations can be difficult to create. Incorporation is often complex and expensive. Corporation organizers must obtain a state-issued **corporate charter** that specifies the corporation's purpose. The corporate charter binds the corporation to its stated objectives and grants it authority to carry out these objectives.

Activities of corporations are restricted and monitored. Corporate charters usually contain broad grants of authority, but sometimes they need to be amended to enable specific activities that were not contemplated when the charter was authorized. Corporations are subject to state and federal laws. Compliance with those laws usually requires extensive records of activities.

Corporate earnings are taxed twice. Corporations pay state and federal taxes on profits. Profits, returned to stockholders in the form of dividends, are taxed again as personal income. Avoidance of double taxation is an advantage of sole proprietorships and partnerships.

Alternative Forms of Ownership

In addition to the primary forms of business ownership already described, alternative forms exist to meet specific needs. Like sole proprietorships and partnerships, some of these entities are unincorporated. The most common ones include the following:

- Professional corporations
- Limited liability companies
- Subchapter S corporations
- Unincorporated associations
- Joint ventures

Professional Corporations

Professional corporations provide professional services, such as those performed by architects, accountants, physicians, or veterinarians. Because those services usually involve the rendering of an expert opinion, legislators historically have been unwilling to shield individuals from liability completely, as usually occurs with incorporation. Professional corporations do not limit the liability of their shareholders for their own professional acts. Such limitation would be contrary to public policy.

Because of changing Internal Revenue Service regulations and favorable court decisions, many states have changed their laws in recent years to allow professional corporations. In states in which these laws exist, an individual or a group of individuals who work in the same profession can form a corporation. For example, a state may allow a lawyer or a group of lawyers to form a professional corporation to practice law; however, this corporation may not include a physician as a shareholder. Many states permit the merger of corporations in similar fields, such as medical and dental corporations. Most professional-corporation laws contain only provisions relevant to professional corporations and refer to the law regarding general business corporations for all other details.

Limited Liability Companies

Limited liability companies (LLCs) are a relatively new organizational form that combine features of partnerships and corporations. As its name suggests, owners or members of an LLC have limited liability for the LLC's obligations and debts. The limited liability of LLCs is analogous to the limited liability granted to shareholders of a corporation. Additionally, LLCs have the same tax advantage of partnerships, in that the LLC's owners and members pay taxes only on profits. LLCs are particularly appealing to those who would otherwise form a partnership to conduct their business.

Subchapter S Corporations

Subchapter S corporations are small business corporations with thirty-five or fewer stockholders.[2] As with LLCs, Subchapter S corporations provide limited liability to their owners and tax treatment similar to that of a partnership.

Unincorporated Associations

Unincorporated associations are voluntary associations of individuals acting together under a common name to achieve a lawful purpose. Unincorporated associations are formed under the common-law right of contract. They have no separate legal existence and technically do not have a perpetual life. Members of an unincorporated association are not generally held liable for actions of the association unless they approved the action or participated in the commission of a tort by the association.

The unincorporated association might have formal articles of association, or a charter, and bylaws. The sharing of expenses and profits in an association is often done on a basis other than per capita. The individual members of an unincorporated association do not have the authority to participate directly in its day-to-day management. An elected board of directors or trustees usually holds that power. Federal tax laws treat an association as a partnership if it resembles a partnership more than a corporation.

A joint venture is a common type of unincorporated association that underwriters are likely to encounter. Other unincorporated associations include trade associations, labor unions, limited partnership associations, clubs, and condominium associations.

Joint Ventures

Joint ventures are unincorporated associations of two or more entities that undertake a specific transaction or activity of usually limited duration. Corporations, partnerships, and sole proprietorships can be members of a joint venture. Many of the general rules governing partnerships apply also to joint ventures. For example, members of a joint venture have unlimited liability during the duration of the joint venture. Large construction projects are often undertaken by a joint venture of contractors.

Other Unincorporated Associations

Trade associations constitute one of the largest groups of other unincorporated associations. The United States has more than 10,000 trade associations, including local and area boards of trade, chambers of commerce, and other business organizations. Trade associations compile and exchange information, lobby legislators, and act to foster the interests of their members. Corporations can also be members.

Labor unions are associations formed to negotiate with employers on behalf of a collective bargaining unit regarding wages, benefits, and working conditions.

The **limited partnership association** is a hybrid organizational form. Like a corporation, it limits the liability of its members and lets them sell their shares. As in a partnership, members retain the right to choose their associates. When a member sells his or her shares, the other members may reject the new member and buy out the interest. Limited partnership associations often own real estate and professional sports franchises.

A **club** is an association of persons who meet or live together for a social purpose or some other common aim, such as the pursuit of literature, science, or politics. Most clubs operate as unincorporated associations. As with an association member, a club member is only liable on a contract that was authorized expressly or by implication.

A **condominium association** cares for the common interests of individuals with an ownership in a condominium. Most condominiums operate as unincorporated associations, although condominium associations can incorporate.

Who Should Be an Insured?

Underwriters must often consider the legal interests of insurance applicants in determining whether to provide insurance coverage. Usually, the applicant has an insurable interest that is easy to identify and evaluate. In other cases, however, the insurance applicant or another party seeking insured status has a less defined legal interest that must be considered carefully.

Insureds have rights—and sometimes responsibilities—under the insurance policy. **Named insureds** are individuals and organizations to which insurance coverage is expressly provided. Named insureds are listed on the declarations page of the insurance policy. In addition, insurance policies often extend insured status to others as part of the insurance coverage. Employees, real estate managers, legal representatives, and newly acquired organizations, for example, are extended insured status in certain circumstances. Underwriters also receive requests from the insurance applicant to add other parties to the policy as additional insureds. Underwriting issues regarding insured status are described in the following sections.

> **First Named Insured**
>
> The **first named insured** is the named insured whose name appears first on the declarations page. Some policy forms obligate the insurer to notify only the first named insured of cancellation and nonrenewal. These policy forms also specify that some of the insured's duties, such as requesting policy cancellation, apply only to the first named insured. The first named insured is entitled to receive any premium refund and to make changes in the policy.
>
> Many insurers turned to this practice of designating and communicating exclusively with the first named insured when keeping up with all the individuals and entities as insureds became impractical. Prior to the use of the first named insured, insurers were obligated to communicate with each insured listed in the policy. An insurer's failure to provide notice of cancellation to an insured meant that the insurer had not legally canceled the policy.

Insuring Ownership Interests

Underwriters can conclude much about the applicant based on the ownership form of the business. The agent or broker completing an ACORD commercial insurance application, as well as many insurer-specific commercial applications, must check a box indicating the applicant's ownership form. The applicant's ownership form should provide the underwriter with a sense of the account's size, scope, and sophistication.

> **ACORD**
>
> Agency-Company Operations Research and Development (ACORD) is a nonprofit organization founded in 1970 to develop and maintain standard application and claim forms. ACORD extended its influence on insurance transactions to include standard formats for the electronic exchange of information among agents, vendors, and insurers. ACORD standards have helped eliminate duplicate paperwork and workflow inefficiencies, thereby reducing insurance costs and enabling insurers to improve customer service.[3]

Sole Proprietorships

There is no legal distinction between a sole proprietorship and its owner. The name of the business owner can be listed alone. More commonly, however, the name of the owner and that of the business are listed together on the declarations page of the insurance policy. It is common practice to list a sole proprietor and his or her business in one the following three ways or in another manner specified by underwriting guidelines:

- "John Jones d/b/a Westtown Plumbing." The letters d/b/a mean "doing business as." This abbreviation identifies a business that appears to be separate from its owner.
- "John Jones t/a Westtown Plumbing." The abbreviation *t/a* means "trading as." The original purpose for this abbreviation was to identify a trade name an individual had adopted.
- "John Jones a/k/a Westtown Plumbing." The abbreviation *a/k/a* ("also known as") allows a person to include in the policy a fictitious name that has been registered with the state. This is a legitimate practice that might mean nothing more than that the insured's real name does not suit the business. For example, Thomas Paine might want to conduct his business under another name if he is a dentist.

> ### Businesses Operating Under Fictitious Names
>
> Many states have fictitious-name acts that require individuals, partnerships, and corporations conducting business under an assumed or fictitious name to register that name with the state.
>
> A fictitious name is any assumed name or designation other than the proper name of the entity using such name. The surname of a person, standing alone or coupled with words that describe the business, is not a fictitious business name. The inclusion of words that suggest additional owners, such as "Company," "& Company," "& Sons," "& Associates," makes the name an assumed or fictitious name. For partnerships, the last name of all partners must be listed, or the fictitious name rule applies.

Insurers derive several benefits from including the name of the owner along with the business name. The sole proprietor-insured might be the owner of other businesses in addition to the one being insured. Having both the owner and the business name listed on the declarations page makes it clear to whom the insurer is providing coverage.

Insureds sometimes mistakenly believe that the insurance on their property transfers with it when the property is sold. Assigning the ownership of an insurance policy is possible but only with the consent of the insurer. In most instances, insurers prefer to write a new insurance policy for the new owner. Underwriters are as interested in the qualities of the owner as they are in those of the property being insured. Having the name of the owner and the business listed together might cause an owner who is transferring the insured property to realize that the policy cannot be transferred directly to the purchaser.

Commercial insurance policies often extend some coverage to newly acquired or constructed locations and newly acquired organizations if certain conditions are met. Naming the business along with the owner might alert the business owner to contact his or her insurer when new properties, new construction, and new ventures are added so that extension of coverage provisions of the policy are not tested by a claim.

Partnerships

A partnership, at one time, was not considered to be a legal entity separate from its owners. Partnership interests were insured by listing all of the partners. Partnerships are now considered to be separate legal entities for many activities, including purchasing insurance. Many agents and brokers, as well as the insurers they represent, continue to identify the partnership and its partners on the policy declarations page.

Underwriters sometimes find that knowing who the individual partners are in a small partnership is just as important as knowing who the owner is in a sole proprietorship. Each partner in a small partnership will likely have a significant role in the partnership's management. Membership changes in a small partnership might change the character of the insured organization.

The partners and their partnership can be named in a policy in any of three common ways. If John Jones and Harry Smith form a partnership named "Smith and Jones General Merchandise," the named insured might be listed as one of the following:

- "John Jones and Harry Smith d/b/a Smith and Jones General Merchandise"
- "Smith and Jones General Merchandise, a partnership consisting of John Jones and Harry Smith"
- "Smith and Jones General Merchandise, John Jones and Harry Smith as partners"

Although identifying individual partners on the declarations page is optional, specifying the partnership is essential. Naming the partnership along with the individual partners clarifies which enterprise is being insured. An individual partner, for example, should not be able to access liability coverage from one enterprise to protect himself or herself for a negligent act associated with another owned business. Underwriters should clearly designate in the declarations the name of the partnership that the insurer is insuring.

Unincorporated Associations

Unincorporated associations are often listed on the declarations in their name alone. If the unincorporated association has subsidiaries, then the declarations will likely specify that all entities are named insureds. For joint ventures, each participant is usually identified on the declarations such as in the approaches taken below:

- "Jones Concrete Corp. and Smith Construction, Inc., d/b/a Main Street Development Associates"
- "Main Street Development Associates, a joint venture of Jones Concrete Corp. and Smith Construction, Inc."
- "Main Street Development Associates, Jones Concrete Corp. and Smith Construction, Inc., as joint adventurers"

These entries identify both the joint venture and its members. In most cases, the members of a joint venture are a more important underwriting factor than are the members of a partnership. The viability of the joint project depends on their combined expertise and financial resources. Substituting one member for another usually has less effect on a partnership than on a joint venture.

Corporations

Because a corporation has an identity that is separate from that of its owners, the name of the corporation should appear on the declarations page. Insuring corporations is sometimes made more complex because one corporation can own other corporations. Corporations should identify all their subsidiaries on the policy declarations page unless they are otherwise insured.

Underwriters often want to know about corporate subsidiaries insured elsewhere because of the possibility of the insured corporation's being included in a lawsuit aimed at a subsidiary. Corporate risk managers sometimes find it advantageous to place insurance for the business with different insurers. Underwriters should specify the entities being insured in such a way that coverage will not be extended to the subsidiaries that are insured elsewhere.

Insuring Multiple Interests

Underwriters are sometimes asked to consider insuring the multiple interests of *one* individual or entity in *one* policy. In other instances, an underwriter might be asked to insure *multiple* individuals and entities with *one* policy. The sections below highlight the factors an underwriter should consider when evaluating these requests.

Multiple Interests of One Individual or Entity

One individual or entity with a controlling interest in other entities might want all its interests insured in one policy. Such requests should be evaluated on a case-by-case basis and with reference to the insurer's underwriting guidelines. An insurer's underwriting guidelines might identify ownership relationships that would be acceptable and specify how extensive the insured's controlling interest must be for inclusion in a single policy. Examples of multiple ownership interests of one individual or entity include the following:

- One person might own a majority interest in several firms. The firms might include more than one form of organization. The sole proprietor of one business might be a majority owner of a partnership or joint venture. The same person could own all or most of the stock of a corporation.

- One business might own all or a majority of other businesses. This practice is common among corporations. A partnership or joint venture might also own another firm.

- One business might operate another under contract with its owners. This is common practice in real estate management. A real estate agent might undertake the management of a number of properties. A separate corporation might own each building, and the real estate manager controls those properties as part of the package.

In some instances, the insured might be unaware that its efforts to simplify its insurance program have caused several entities to share coverage limits. Unless higher coverage limits are purchased, the insured might have less insurance coverage than if separate policies had been purchased.

Insuring Different Controlling Interests

Businesses that do not have common owners sometimes need insurance for joint operation such as a joint venture. A similar need exists when one business contracts with another to perform certain operations and wants to add the other party to its insurance policy as an additional insured.

Identifying and addressing different interests are less of a problem in property insurance than in liability insurance. Property policies describe the property to which the coverage applies. The policies limit recovery to each party's insurable interest. Liability insurance coverage forms, on the other hand, do not try to measure insurable interest, but rather give complete protection to each party named as an insured. Although liability forms are designed to provide necessary coverage, they might also provide duplicate coverage.

Designing an appropriate insurance program requires an understanding of both the operations that the insured performs jointly with others and those that it handles alone. Many parties that engage in joint operations with others choose to insure their joint operations under a joint policy that is separate from each party's individual policy.

Wrap-ups

Wrap-ups are risk management programs specifically designed for large construction projects. The project sponsor—usually the owner or general contractor—purchases selected insurance coverages for all contractors and subcontractors working on the project. Participating contractors are able to reduce their contract bid by the amount they would have paid for coverage provided by the sponsor's wrap-up. Wrap-ups are marketed under various names, including owner controlled insurance programs, controlled construction insurance programs, and consolidated insurance programs. Wraps-ups have proven to be an efficient and cost-effective approach to handling construction-related insurance needs for project sponsors.

Various coverages can be included in a wrap-up. Usually, a wrap-up will include workers compensation and general liability insurance. Optional coverages that might be included in the program are builders risk, environmental liability, asbestos abatement, and architects and engineers errors and omissions. Wrap-ups usually do not include commercial auto coverage, nor do they usually cover suppliers and vendors as insureds.

Contractors participating in a wrap-up likely have insurance for their other operations, and that insurance should exclude coverage for activities covered by the wrap-up. The ISO endorsement entitled *Exclusion—Designated Operations Covered By A Consolidated (Wrap-Up) Insurance Program* (CG 21 54) eliminates coverage from the participating contractor's CGL policy for designated operations and locations listed in the endorsement. The NCCI endorsement entitled *Designated Workplaces Exclusion Endorsement* (WC 00 03 02) performs this task for the Standard Workers Compensation and Employers Liability Insurance Policy.

Wrap-ups are usually reserved for large construction projects, but it is the insurer's underwriting guidelines that specify eligibility. Although wrap-ups could be used for any construction project that involves more than one contractor, the administrative costs associated with wrap-ups cause most insurers to establish a significant minimum premium requirement.

Advantages of Wrap-Ups

Wrap-ups enable one insurer to cost-effectively provide loss control services.

Construction projects involve hazardous activities, such as blasting and excavation. The need to coordinate the efforts of several contractors on a work site increases the likelihood that hazardous activities will cause bodily injury and property damage to workers or the public. Loss control can be very effective in controlling construction-related losses, but these services come with a cost. Wrap-ups permit a coordinated approach to loss control that cannot be afforded if the premium paid by the participating contractors were going to several insurers instead of the one providing the wrap-up.

Wrap-ups enable the project sponsor to negotiate a volume discount on the consolidated insurance costs of a construction project. A large construction project will usually generate a significant premium. Insurers are usually willing to discount the premium that would otherwise be charged to write the account. Large accounts justify insurer loss control efforts because loss savings created by these efforts are usually apparent. Premium discounts are justified because the savings from loss control efforts can usually more than compensate for premium reductions.

Wrap-ups reduce disputes between parties. When a loss occurs, it is often difficult to identify one contractor who is solely responsible for causing it. Because the same insurer insures all the participating contractors in a wrap-up, the need to assign fault to particular contractors does not exist as it would if no wrap-up were used. Wrap-ups eliminate animosity that might be created between contractors when fault is assigned to one contractor, even though many contractors had a hand in causing the loss.

Wrap-ups provide a uniform insurance program for the project sponsor and participating contractors. Without the wrap-up, some small contractors might have difficulty obtaining liability limits demanded by the property owner or general contractor. Additionally, the wrap-up eliminates the administrative headache of obtaining certificates of insurance from each contractor and of ensuring that aggregate limits of individual contractors and subcontractors remain available to respond to claims.

Disadvantages of Wrap-Ups

Wrap-ups reduce the incentives for contractors to implement safety programs. Because good loss experience is reflected in the experience modification of the project sponsor, participating contractors have only an indirect benefit from their efforts to control losses. Likewise, the combined rating of participating contractors insulates contractors who have worse-than-average loss experience from paying a premium based on their loss history.

A wrap-up's policy limits should be high enough to protect the project sponsor and participating contractors. If the wrap-up's limits are too low, they might be exhausted easily. This possibility increases with the number of participating contractors and the hazardous nature of the work performed at the construction site. If the policy limits prove to be inadequate, participating contractors will have little chance to recover from the at-fault contractor because of the attachment of wrap-up exclusions to the contractors' other policies.

Because much of a participating contractor's insurance needs are addressed in the wrap-up, participating contractors may have difficulty obtaining coverage for the balance of their insurance needs. Wrap-ups often require participating contractors to sever or change the relationship they have established with their agents or brokers.

Insuring Entities Other Than the Named Insured

Extending coverage to parties other than the named insured is a common practice. Liability policies are often endorsed to cover additional insureds, and property policies are often arranged to cover the interests of mortgagees and loss payees. Careless use of either practice, however, can create exposures not anticipated by the insurer.

Additional Insureds in Liability Insurance

Underwriters are often asked to add another party as an additional insured to an insured's liability insurance policy. Additional insureds are granted coverage under the insured's liability policy, but they do not have the same rights and duties as named insureds. In most instances, the insured has either been asked to add another party as an additional insured or has a contractual obligation to do so. ISO developed additional insured endorsements for typical relationships. The attachment of *Additional Insured—Church Members, Officers and Volunteer Workers* (CG 20 22), for example, extends liability coverage to any church member but only with respect to their activities on behalf of the church. This endorsement also extends liability coverage to the church's leaders and clergy, but only with respect to their church-related duties. Other ISO-developed additional insured endorsements are listed in Exhibit 2-1. Underwriters might find it necessary to manuscript an additional insured endorsement to meet the specific needs of an account. If doing so, the underwriter should restrict liability coverage to those claims arising out of the named insured's operations. Underwriters usually perform an in-depth analysis in those instances in which the relationship between the insured and the proposed additional insured has not already been addressed by an existing endorsement. For these requests, underwriters should understand the relationship between the parties and the reason for the request, as well as the potential consequences to the insurer of adding the additional insured.

Exhibit 2-1
ISO-Developed Additional Insured Endorsements

Additional Insured—Club Members

Additional Insured—Concessionaires Trading Under Your Name

Additional Insured—Condominium Unit Owners

Additional Insured—Controlling Interest

Additional Insured—Engineers, Architects, or Surveyors

Additional Insured—Users of Golfmobiles

Additional Insured—Owners, Lessees or Contractors—Scheduled Person or Organization (For Use When Contractual Liability Coverage Is Not Provided to You in This Policy)

Additional Insured—Owners, Lessees or Contractors (Forms A and B)

Additional Insured—Owners, Lessees or Contractors—Scheduled Person or Organization

Additional Insured—Managers or Lessors of Premises

Additional Insured—State or Political Subdivisions—Permits

Additional Insured—State or Political Subdivisions—Permits Relating to Premises

Additional Insured—Users of Teams, Draft or Saddle Animals

Additional Insured—Vendors

Additional Insured—Townhouse Associations

Additional Insured—Mortgagee, Assignee, or Receiver

Additional Insured—Charitable Institutions

Additional Insured—Volunteer Workers

Additional Insured—Volunteers

Additional Insured—Executors, Administrators, Trustees or Beneficiaries

Additional Insured—Owners or Other Interests From Whom Land Has Been Leased

Additional Insured—Elective or Appointive Executive Officers of Public Corporations

Additional Insured—Designated Person or Organization

Additional Insured—Co-owner of Insured Premise

Additional Insured—Lessor of Leased Equipment

Additional Insured—Grantor of Franchise

Additional Insured—Engineers, Architects or Surveyors Not Engaged by the Named Insured

Additional Insured—Owners, Lessees or Contractors—Automatic Status When Required in Construction Agreement With You

Additional Insured—Lessor of Lease Equipment— Automatic Status When Required in Lease Agreement With You

Sometimes the existence of the particular party requesting to be added as an additional insured changes the account's underwriting acceptability. Other than knowledge of a relationship between the insured and the additional insured, the underwriter usually has little information about the liability loss exposure that the additional insured presents. If the underwriter is able to identify correctable problems that present a liability exposure, there is often little the underwriter can do to make the additional insured take corrective action.

Named insureds can become vicariously liable for acts of others. An independent contractor, for example, might be hired to perform work for the insured and injure someone in its performance. It is likely that the injured person will make a claim against both the independent contractor and the named insured. If the independent contractor was added to the policy as an additional insured, the insurer would, at least, know of the independent contractor's activities and receive early notice of the claim.

Most general liability insurance policies are designed to cover the named insured's loss exposure created by independent contractors. However, the named insured sometimes insists that the independent contractor bear the cost of this coverage by purchasing an owners and contractors protective (OCP) liability insurance policy, which is a special form of premises and operations liability insurance that protects the interests of the principal that has hired the independent contractor. The principal (who is the named insured of the OCP policy) can be either a property owner who requires a general contractor to buy the OCP policy, or a general contractor who requires a subcontractor to buy the OCP policy.

Owners and Contractors Protective Liability Insurance

ISO's Owners and Contractors Protective Liability Coverage Form (CG 00 09) provides coverage for bodily injury or property damage arising out of either (1) operations performed for the named insured by the designated contractor at the location specified in the policy or (2) the named insured's own acts or omissions in connection with the "general supervision" of the designated contractor's operations.

The OCP policy's other insurance clause states that it is primary and will not seek recovery from other policies. Should the OCP occurrence or aggregate limit be exhausted, the named insured's CGL coverage form will respond.

Many insurers make an incidental premium charge for adding an additional insured. This premium offsets some of the administrative costs and might discourage some insureds from requesting that additional insureds be added when they are not obligated to do so.

Additional insureds are sometimes aggressive in their demands of the insurer. Additional insureds, in some instances, request that coverage forms be modified to their specifications or that they be notified of any material changes in the insured's coverage, as well as any notice of nonrenewal or cancellation the insurer might issue. Many insurers have information systems and procedures to accommodate these types of requests so that the contractual obligations to the additional insured do not mistakenly extend after the named insured's policy is canceled.

Loss Payees and Mortgageholders in Property Insurance

Underwriters regularly honor insureds' requests to add loss payees and mortgageholders to property policies. Lenders have an insurable interest in property used as collateral to the extent of the unpaid balance on the named insured's loan. Rather than purchasing their own policy or having the property owner purchase one on their behalf, lenders' interests are recognized in the borrower's policy.

Lenders with a security interest in *personal* property, owners of property leased to the insured, and purchasers or sellers under a contract of sale can have their interests protected through a loss payable endorsement. The ISO endorsement entitled *Loss Payable Provisions* (CP 12 18) has space to describe the property, as well as three sets of provisions—loss payable, lender's loss payable, and contract of sale. The loss payable provision in this endorsement only provides the loss payee the right to have payments for any loss made jointly to the loss payee and the insured. The lender's loss payable provision in this endorsement provides the loss payee with rights similar to those of a mortgageholder, described below. An entry in the endorsement or on the declarations indicates the provisions that apply.

Mortgageholders have a secured interest in *real* property. Most property policies provide mortgageholders with rights separate from those of the insured through policy provisions. Mortgageholder provisions are designed to preclude the need of mortgageholders to purchase a separate policy by providing them with rights independent of the insured's. The ISO *Business and Personal Property Coverage Form* includes provisions protecting mortgageholder interests' designated of those mortgageholders listed in the declarations.

Adding loss payees and mortgageholders to a property policy does not raise the same kind of underwriting concerns that naming an additional insured on a liability policy does. Because property policies permit recovery only to the extent of each party's insurable interest, insurer payments in excess of the amount of loss are unlikely. If, however, an insurer erroneously pays a loss directly to the named insured without honoring the rights of the mortgageholder, the insurer will be liable to the mortgageholder to the extent of its interests.

Underwriting the Management of the Organization

The insured's management is one of the most important underwriting characteristics of an account, but one of the most difficult for the underwriter to evaluate. Well-managed businesses are not only earning profits for their owners; they are also operating in an organized and predictable manner so that circumstances that might lead to a loss are avoided or controlled. Experienced managers, for example, know which tasks are hazardous and what precautions should be taken to ensure the safety of employees and the public. The features that make an insured's management desirable are often difficult for the underwriter to determine from the insurance application alone.

Perhaps the most tangible measure of management quality is the financial results a business produces. Measures of financial performance are discussed in Chapter 4. Underwriters can, however, assess the qualitative characteristics of an account's management through information provided on loss control reports, premium audit reports, claim files, information provided by the producer, and the underwriter's first-hand knowledge of the account. Amalgamating information in this manner is a less than perfect approach, but it is often the most realistic way for an underwriter to obtain insight into the account's management ability and assess it.

Ability and Experience

Management ability consists of the knowledge and application of proper administrative methods to the particular business. It involves planning, organizing, motivating employees, and controlling operations. Completing jobs on schedule, keeping job costs within original estimates, delivering goods on time, and operating at a profit comparable to others in the same business are signs of a well-managed business.

Experience is another factor to consider when evaluating how well the organization performs. The length of time that management personnel have been in business and their type of experience are good indicators of competence. Working for others, for example, develops basic techniques and expertise. Operating one's own business develops managerial ability.

Reputation

Business reputation is a gauge of the insured's conduct. Well-managed accounts are sensitive to what the public and their peers think about the business because it is their reputation that will likely affect the amount of business they receive in the future. A poor reputation might be evidenced by how frequently work has to be corrected (callbacks) or the number of complaints made about the business with the Better Business Bureau.

Quality of Work

Quality of work directly affects the product or service provided. Quality products and careful attention to services performed are expected of any legitimate business organization. Shoddy work or service might be evidence of poor supervisory and management attitudes and the insured's overall competence. Past claims might demonstrate that faulty products or inferior work has led to bodily injury and property damage claims.

Prudence of Operations

Prudence of operations indicates the organization's ability to conduct its operations within the limits of its capabilities. Expanding too rapidly or branching into a new area might overextend resources and abilities, as well as management talent. Operations that are unusual for the insured's classification might alert the underwriter that the insured has undertaken a new venture that might stretch the insured's resources.

Employees

Quality accounts usually have quality employees. Owners and managers usually rely on their employees to conduct the operation of the business properly even in their absence. Quality employees are experienced, trained, adequately compensated, and usually full time.

Experience

Experienced employees know how to perform the tasks expected of them. Generally, experienced employees need less supervision than inexperienced employees, and the products that experienced employees produce or services they render will not only satisfy the customer, but the product or work will be less likely to lead to an insurance claim. Employee experience can be measured by the average length of time the employees have been in the business.

Longevity with the account is another measure of employee experience that has an additional benefit of indicating the level of employee loyalty the account might have.

Training

Trained employees know how the owner or manager wants the business conducted. Experience and training are related; effective training can often shorten the learning time needed to perform the job that experience might eventually provide. Accounts that train their employees in new processes and procedures are more likely to train them to approach their jobs in ways that might reduce the frequency and severity of losses. Accounts often demonstrate their commitment to training by conducting regular safety meetings. At these meetings, management representatives reinforce the importance of safety procedures, describe changes in the work that might increase its danger, and review mistakes that have led to injuries. Trained employees are prepared to address workplace challenges whether they are safety-related or not.

Adequate Compensation

Adequate compensation allows a business to attract and keep good workers. Good wages are a major factor in reducing employee turnover. Compensation includes employee benefits, such as health insurance, life insurance, retirement plans, vacation, and sick pay, as well as wages. Employers' compensation programs can increase employee morale and loyalty. Competition for skilled workers is keen in tight labor markets; underwriters prefer accounts that employ average or above-average employees. Because some insurance coverages use payroll as the basis for premium determination, low wages relative to the norm might mean that the insurer is receiving a lower premium relative to the exposure assumed.

Many businesses employ unionized workers whose wages are set by contract. Many unions have apprentice and training programs that usually ensure that employees can perform adequately. In some trades, however, the local unions are able to assign workers without the employer having discretion over who is hired. Underwriters should know whether an account relies on union labor because past poor labor relations have led to situations in which thefts and vandalism losses have occurred.

Full-time

Extensive use of part-time rather than full-time employees was once considered a negative attribute of an account because full-time employees were thought to be better trained. Employment practices have changed, and many employers make extensive use of part-time employees. Many businesses are seasonal or have daily peak work periods that make hiring full-time employees impractical. For accounts in which the ratio of full-time to part-time employees seems inappropriate, underwriters should consider whether an extensive reliance on part-time employees might increase the account's exposure to loss.

Risk Management

Risk management is the process of making and implementing decisions that will minimize the adverse effects of accidental and business losses on an organization. The steps in the risk management decision-making process are similar to those of the underwriting decision-making process described in Chapter 1. Implementing these decisions requires the risk manager to perform the four functions in the management process: planning, organizing, leading, and controlling resources.

Risk Management Decision-Making Process

1. Identify and analyze exposures and business losses that might interfere with an organization's basic objectives.

2. Examine feasible alternative risk management techniques for dealing with those exposures.

3. Select the apparently best risk management techniques.

4. Implement the chosen risk management techniques.

5. Monitor the results of the chosen techniques to ensure that the risk management program remains effective.[4]

Many business organizations make use of risk management. The larger the business, the more likely that the risk management function will be formalized and an employee or employees will be assigned to that task. Many of the largest U.S. corporations have large risk management departments that are involved in risk management techniques other than insurance, such as retention, noninsurance transfer, and loss control. In a sole proprietorship, on the other hand, the owner acting on the advice of an insurance agent or broker usually performs the risk-management function. Many businesses rely on firms that provide risk management services or risk management consultants.

Underwriters generally recognize that risk management programs are implemented in different degrees. In some organizations, the risk manager has extensive authority and is part of, or reports directly to, top management. In other organizations, the risk management program exists in name only and the risk manager's role is limited to purchasing insurance for the organization. Having a risk management program in place is a positive attribute of an account. However, underwriters often need to determine whether the risk manager has the authority to make changes that could potentially control the frequency and severity of losses.

Operational Authority

Some accounts exercise extensive operational authority over their sub-operating units, while other accounts permit operating units to operate independently. Accounts that operate through branch or regional offices, or that operate separate plants may dictate practices and procedures used in day-to-day operations, or they may permit the business units to operate autonomously. Likewise, franchises may have freedom to make changes in their operations or be restricted by their franchise agreement to specific practices and materials. Underwriters want to know whether the entity that is making commitments to loss control recommendations has the authority to implement them.

Underwriting and Employment Relationships

Employees obviously play a vital role in an insured's operations. Regardless of the insured's legal structure, processing techniques, managerial skills, or financial condition, the people working for the insured contribute the most to the success or failure of the enterprise. In reviewing the insured's operations, the underwriter should scrutinize each stage of the process and note who performs the work. Sometimes businesses engage independent contractors to carry out some phase of the operation. However, the distinction between employees and independent contractors is not always clear. Sometimes, more than one organization might be considered the employer of a particular person. A careful analysis of who performs the insured's operations contributes to a better understanding of the business, provides significant underwriting information, and allows the underwriter to develop the appropriate premium.

The underwriter must consider the contributions of employees to the final product or service in determining what insurance coverage applies. The insured's liability might depend on whether the person involved in an accident has the status of employee or independent contractor. Even if the insured is liable for a loss, the insurer will only pay for the loss if the insured has the appropriate coverage for the situation.

The underwriting value of this information depends on the coverage being provided. For example, if a products or completed operations exposure is involved, the underwriter wants to know how much control the insured has over the people doing the work. Unless the insured enforces strict quality control standards, the chance of loss might be greater when part-time employees or independent contractors perform the work. If the insurer provides workers compensation coverage, the insured's hiring and training practices are important to the underwriter. The success of a loss control program might depend on whether the insured has an employer's normal authority to control the working environment.

The status of individuals working for the insured might also have an important bearing on the basis of premium. For workers compensation policies, the question of employment status is crucial. The premium base includes the remuneration for every person considered an employee under workers compensation laws, which apply a broad definition of employee. Remuneration is often the premium basis for other coverages, although some of those considered employees for workers compensation purposes might not be counted as employees for other kinds of insurance.

Employment

Employment is a condition in which one person agrees to provide services for another in return for wages or some other form of consideration. An **employee** is a person hired to perform services for another under the direction and control of that other person, called the **employer**. The employee-employer relationship is a contractual one, and valid employment contracts have the same essential elements as all binding contracts. The definition of "employment" presumes the existence of either an express or an implied **contract of hire**. Each party must agree to the arrangement, and each party must have a reasonable expectation of deriving a benefit. Although its effect has been altered by statute in certain circumstances, this principle is often cited to resolve ambiguous situations. The element of consideration is particularly significant in employment contracts. The employee provides labor services, and the employer provides wages, salary, or something else of value. The existence of some form of consideration can be crucial in the underwriter's determination of whether an individual is an employee. Disputed cases are examined to see whether a valid contract of hire exists.

Employers are obligated to compensate their employees for the services performed. An employer who discharges an employee must generally pay wages through the expiration of the last pay period. Many contracts even provide for severance pay or some other compensation for an additional period. Either party may terminate an employment contract by giving notice to the other, although limitations apply. Some state laws and most union contracts specify the period of notice an employer must give an employee. Some employees, such as public school teachers or civil service workers, cannot be discharged without a hearing. Employees wrongfully discharged can bring action against the employer under federal or state labor relation laws.

There is little disagreement concerning the employment definition and the associated legal principles presented above. Applying the definition to particular borderline situations, however, often becomes a problem. As one authority has noted:

> The definition of the term "employee" for purposes of vicarious liability, employer's liability, workmen's compensation, labor legislation, unemployment compensation, social security and miscellaneous enactments applicable to employees, has probably produced more reported cases than any definition of status in the modern history of law.[5]

The definition problem is further complicated by the fact that a person who is an employee for one of the above purposes is not necessarily considered an employee for the other purposes. An employee for federal tax purposes might not be an employee for insurance purposes. Whether a particular person is an employee depends on the context in which the question arises.

Many small and medium-sized companies lease employees from **professional employer organizations (PEOs)** in an effort to improve their benefits and reduce costs. These companies may have no employees, or they may directly employ only their top executives. In a typical scenario, a company (the client) will transfer all or most of its existing employees to a PEO and lease them back.

All or most of the workers in these cases are direct employees of the PEO. The client-company for which they actually do their work is an indirect employer. Companies have used the services of labor contractors for temporary and casual employees for years. What makes the newer arrangements different from contract labor is that companies lease their permanent work force from a third-party leasing company.

Under workers compensation laws, leased employees are generally considered employees of both the PEO and its client. Both the direct and the indirect employer have an obligation to provide workers compensation benefits, and the exclusive remedy doctrine protects both employers. NCCI and state workers compensation boards have revised workers compensation forms to address the issue of dual employment.

The fact that an insured leases a substantial number of employees cannot be overlooked by the underwriter. In most instances, the PEO provides workers compensation coverage. This may not create a problem if the indirect employer leases all employees and does not carry workers compensation coverage. However, a company that leases employees will often remain the direct employer of top executives. This is especially true of sole proprietorships, partnerships, limited liability companies, and closely held corporations. Proprietors and partners may not be subject to the workers compensation law, but they may elect coverage in most states. If the indirect employer carries workers compensation coverage, its carrier will become liable for claims by leased employees if the PEO does not have insurance. Underwriters should verify that the proper coverage is in place at policy inception and at each renewal. They should also investigate the reputation of the PEO the insured uses. Most PEOs are highly reputable firms, but there have been some examples of fraud in this industry.

Independent Contractors

Normally, a business can accomplish a particular task in only one of two ways. Either it can hire an employee to perform the task, or it can contract with an independent contractor. An independent contractor usually makes a business of providing a certain service to several different customers. An independent contractor, however, need not work for more than one customer. The nature of the relationship between the two parties determines who is an independent contractor.

Just as employees and their actions are a concern of the commercial underwriter, so are independent contractors and their actions. An injury to an employee of an uninsured independent contractor can result in a workers compensation claim under the policy of the organization engaging that contractor. In some situations, that same organization's general liability policy might be called on to respond to damages resulting from the actions of an independent contractor. Determining whether an individual is an employee or independent contractor is just not a matter of determining the degree of liability. The determination relates to the nature of the exposure presented and the alternatives available to the underwriter in treating that exposure.

Characteristics of Independent Contractors

An independent contractor often receives compensation in a lump sum, sometimes after submitting a bill for services. The bill might itemize the cost of labor and materials, but it does not have to segregate those costs if the contract simply sets a price for the completion of the job. Although the parties might agree on terms for payment and specifications for the project, an independent contractor works under an ordinary contract in which one party promises a certain sum of money in return for the other party's performance of work.

Unlike employees, independent contractors are not subject to direction and control regarding the details of the work. They agree to perform a task meeting the specifications stipulated in the contract, but they are free to use their own judgment and methods in performing the task. They can also employ others to perform the task, but they remain responsible under the contract for its completion.

An employee whose work is unsatisfactory may be discharged. When an independent contractor's work is unsatisfactory, the usual recourse is to sue for breach of contract. Unless the breach can be proved, the other party must pay the independent contractor the sum specified in the contract.

Independent contractors usually offer services to the public. Large firms can normally be readily identified as independent contractors, but smaller ones are harder to judge. Such factors as a commercial telephone listing, printed invoices, incorporation, commercial insurance coverage, and a separate place of business can be evidence of independent status.

Reasons for Using Independent Contractors

Independent contractors often provide a service involving some measure of specialization. Sometimes the specialized service requires a high degree of knowledge and skill, perhaps even professional training and licensing. Public accountants, for example, often keep the books for small businesses because the owners do not have the necessary knowledge of accounting principles and cannot afford to hire a full-time employee who does. Similarly, attorneys, architects, or other professionals might offer their services for a particular case or project.

In other situations, independent contractors have the specialized equipment or facilities to perform particular tasks at a lower cost. Businesses of all sizes, for example, find contracting with a trash removal firm to pick up the trash easier than assigning an employee to drive the trash to the dump in the same van the company uses for deliveries to customers.

Businesses often employ independent contractors to transfer an exposure to someone else. A manufacturer who produces hazardous wastes, for example, could conceivably contract directly with a hazardous-waste site for disposal. Most organizations, however, engage the services of a hazardous-waste hauler to transport the wastes to the disposal site. The potential liability for accidents in transit is a major factor in this decision. Many real estate agents are capable of performing simple home inspections for clients. They nevertheless engage the services of a professional home inspector. Avoiding the errors and omissions exposure is often the primary reason for the decision to use an independent contractor for these types of functions.

Specialists can better handle other infrequent situations. For example, if a company holds an annual banquet to honor its top salespeople, it may have a caterer provide the food.

Although many kinds of work involve independent contractors, the occupation itself does not make a person or firm an independent contractor. An attorney can represent a client as an independent contractor or perform exactly the same services as a full-time employee. As another example, if a homeowner contracts with a plumber to repair bathroom plumbing, the plumber would be considered an independent contractor. If a home builder engaged the same plumber to install bathrooms of the same type in many new homes, the plumber might be an employee, particularly if the builder paid the plumber by the hour, supervised the work, and had the right to discharge the plumber at any time during the construction.[6]

Finally, independent contractors are often used to avoid the costs associated with employees. Independent contractors require no payroll taxes or benefits. For these reasons, underwriters encounter situations in which an organization refers to a certain worker as an independent contractor rather than as an employee. Yet according to most definitions, and for insurance purposes, the person is really an employee. The underwriter must therefore be able to distinguish between what the organization calls that person and the actual relationship between that person and the organization. Typically, the latter gives a true indication of a person's employment status.

General Contractors and Subcontractors

Independent contractor relationships become more confusing when there is a hierarchy of such relationships. One person might contract a project to another person, who might contract a portion of the work to a third person. In such cases, the terms "general contractor" and "subcontractor" are commonly used to distinguish the parties. Such distinctions might clarify the hierarchy on a particular job, but both general contractors and subcontractors are independent contractors.

A **general contractor** is an independent contractor who obtains the primary contract for a project and either completes all the work or subcontracts certain portions, or all of the work, to other independent contractors who specialize in such work. Although subcontracting occurs most often in the construction industry, it is also common in manufacturing and publishing. Contractors who subcontract all their work to others are often referred to as **paper contractors**.

Subcontractors, or specialty contractors, are independent contractors who specialize in a particular kind of work. They are engaged by a general contractor to perform a particular portion of the general contractor's contract. Plumbers and electricians, for example, might be subcontractors on a building construction project. At other times, however, they might work directly for a property owner instead of having a general contractor as an intermediary.

Tests of Employer-Employee Relationships in a Legal Context

When an employment issue is in dispute, a court or other administrative body with jurisdiction in the area of employment relationships would decide the case. However, certain factors are particularly significant in determining whether an employment relationship exists. The traditional test has been whether the alleged employer has the right to direct and control the work. Decisions have also been based on the relative nature of the work. Underwriters should understand the reasoning involved in each of these tests of employment status, even though only the appropriate judicial body can resolve the question. The following sections present only a brief discussion of the tests of employment status.

Direction and Control

The common-law test of an employer-employee relationship is the employer's right to direct and control the employee. As one court stated,

> Generally, when a person for whom services are performed has the right to control and direct the individual who performs the services not only as to the result to be accomplished by the worker but also to the details and the means by which the result is accomplished, the individual subject to direction is an employee.[7]

Relative Nature of the Work

The element of control emphasized in the common-law test of employment status relates to the employer's liability to third parties and is less relevant in other contexts. In applying social and labor legislation, courts tend to define employee status in such a way as to provide the protection of those laws to the people who need it.[8] Since the direction and control test can be subject to differences of opinion, courts also examine the economic reality of the employer-employee relationship. This "relative nature of the work" test assumes particular importance in workers compensation cases. In such cases, injured workers might qualify for benefits because they are economically dependent on the alleged employer even though they are not subject to direction and control. Because of their economic dependence, such individuals would have no protection unless they were extended the benefits of the workers compensation law.

Underwriting and the Insured's Business Category

Underwriters need to know exactly the type of work the insured performs. Additionally, underwriters need to know whether the insured's operations are consistent with other accounts sharing the same classification. The approach to underwriting suggested by this text requires that underwriters *investigate* as well as *evaluate* accounts. An experienced underwriter, for example, knows to ask more questions when the application simply indicates the insured is a "contractor." Guides, such as *Best's Underwriting Guide*, are available to help underwriters learn more about the business category they are underwriting.

One approach to categorizing commercial accounts is that taken by ISO in Division Six—General Liability of the *Commercial Lines Manual* (CLM). CLM classifications are categorized into the following business groups:

- Manufacturing or processing
- Contracting or servicing
- Mercantile
- Building or premises
- Miscellaneous

Underwriters need to understand these business groups to properly classify and price accounts for general liability coverage. ISO's classification system, however, is not particularly informative of the range of accounts that can be placed in each of its classifications. Many insurers encourage their underwriters to use the North American Industry Classification System (NAICS) to gain a broader understanding of accounts.

The **North American Industry Classification System (NAICS)**, developed jointly by the United States, Mexico, and Canada, is a comprehensive taxonomy of business activities. NAICS began supplanting the U.S. Standard Industrial Classification (SIC) system in 1997. The NAICS classifies all economic activities into twenty sectors. NAICS sector codes and sectors are listed in Exhibit 2-2.[9]

Underwriters find the NAICS codes useful in gaining an understanding of the insured's business activities and those of related businesses. A commercial application might state, for example, that the nature of an insured's business is that of a "baker." Brief information, such as this, is typical of types of responses underwriters receive on commercial applications. If the underwriter working on this account were to look up "baker" in the *CLM Classification Table*, he

Exhibit 2-2

North American Industry Classification System Sectors

Code	Sector
11	Agriculture, Forestry, Fishing, and Hunting
21	Mining
22	Utilities
23	Construction
31-33	Manufacturing
41-43	Wholesale Trade
44-46	Retail Trade
48-49	Transportation and Warehousing
51	Information
52	Finance and Insurance
53	Real Estate and Rental and Leasing
54	Professional, Scientific, and Technical Services
55	Management of Companies and Enterprises
56	Administrative and Support and Waste Management and Remediation Services
61	Educational Services
62	Health Care and Social Assistance
71	Arts, Entertainment, and Recreation
72	Accommodations and Food Services
81	Other Services (except Public Administration)
91-93	Public Administration

The NAICS uses a six-digit code structure to classify specific business operations:

First two digits	Sector code
Third digit	Subsector code
Fourth digit	Industry group
Fifth digit	Industry
Sixth digit	U.S. industry

The sixth digit is used when a country has a need to further classify a sector. If the sixth digit of U.S. NAICS code is a zero, this digit indicates that no further classification was needed for U.S. industries.

or she would find only two classifications: "bakeries" and "bakery plants." NAICS, on the other hand provides the more detailed information shown in Exhibit 2-3.

Exhibit 2-3
NAICS Bakery Classifications With Retail Bakeries Highlighted

3118   Bakeries and Tortilla Manufacturing

31181   Bread and Bakery Products Manufacturing

311811 Retail Bakeries

This U.S. industry comprises establishments primarily engaged in retailing bread and other bakery products not for immediate consumption made on the premises from flour, not from prepared dough.

Cross-references. Establishments primarily engaged in—

- Retailing bakery products not for immediate consumption made else- where—are classified in U.S. Industry 445291, Baked Goods Stores;

- Preparing and selling bakery products (i.e., cookies, pretzels) for imme- diate consumption—are classified in Industry 722213, Snack and Non- alcoholic Beverage Bars;

- Manufacturing fresh or frozen breads and other fresh bakery (except cookies and crackers) products—are classified in U.S. Industry 311812, Commercial Bakeries; and

- Manufacturing cookies and crackers—are classified in Industry 31182, Cookie, Cracker, and Pasta Manufacturing;

311812 Commercial Bakeries

311813 Frozen Cakes, Pies, and Other Pastries Manufacturing

North American Industry Classification System—United States, 1997, Executive Office of the President, Office of Management and Budget (Lanham, MD: Bernan Press, 1998), pp. 124-125.

Underwriters can use the NAICS to gain additional insight into activities that might be conducted by the insured. By reviewing cross-references, underwrit- ers can also determine activities that the insured likely does not do. The hierarchical approach used by NAICS might help refine underwriters' think- ing about how business activities are usually conducted in any particular industry niche.

An account's NAICS code is not requested on the ACORD commercial insurance application. Some insurers use supplemental applications to capture this and other information they have determined to be relevant. Even if the

NAICS code is not provided by the insured, underwriters will likely benefit from the process of sorting through the printed listing of NAICS codes or the NAICS's Internet search engine.

Summary

Underwriters need to understand an account's operations to be able to assess their exposures to loss. To determine whether the loss exposures of an account are typical for that insured's classification, the underwriter needs to know about the other types of businesses that can be similarly classified. This chapter offers the reader an approach to gauging business ownership, employer practices, and business operations.

The principal types of commercial organizations are sole proprietorships, partnerships, and corporations. The sole proprietorship is the simplest form of business because it is owned by one person who is its manager. A partnership is an association of two or more persons who agree to enter into a business to share in its profits and losses. A corporation is an artificial person created by law to conduct business or carry out another specific purpose. Other forms of business ownership include professional corporations, limited liability companies, subchapter S corporations, membership corporations, and joint ventures. Limited liability companies are a relatively new form of business organization, but they might prove to be a more popular organizational form than partnerships because of the income tax advantages they provide.

Underwriters must make sure the named insured is correctly identified in the policy declarations. Underwriters usually rely on the organizational form of the account and the insurer's underwriting guidelines to ensure that the interests of the insured are properly designated. Additionally, underwriters need to evaluate requests to name multiple operations of one entity in a single policy or name multiple entities with a common interest in a single policy. Wrap-ups are consolidated insurance programs for large construction projects. Wrap-ups address the coverage needs of the project sponsor and participating contractors.

Underwriters regularly receive requests from insureds to add other parties to the policy as additional insureds. In evaluating these requests, the underwriter should understand the relationship between the insured and the proposed additional insured, the reason for the request, and the consequences to the insurer of granting the request.

Underwriters must understand the tests of employer-employee relationships and distinguish between the two. Two common tests used to determine employer-employee relations are the employer's right to direct and control the employee, and the relative nature of the work. Underwriters need an understanding of the structure of employment in particular organizations. If an organization uses independent contractors, the underwriter must know about each contractor (including general contractors and subcontractors) and the insured's reasons for using them.

To evaluate the management of an organization, underwriters must consider its ability and experience, reputation, quality of work, prudence of operations, and employees. The presence of a risk management program at an insured account is a positive attribute. However, underwriters need to evaluate whether the insured's risk management program will really help control losses. An insured's management may not have the authority needed to make changes that would control loss frequency and severity; underwriters need to know if operational procedures are controlled elsewhere.

Experienced underwriters usually have a broad understanding of how businesses operate and how they relate to one another. One way to gain this expertise is to use industry classification guides such as the North American Industry Classification System.

Chapter Notes

1. *Statistical Abstract of the United States 1998*, U.S. Department of Commerce, Table 855, p. 540.
2. Subchapter S corporations get their name from the section of the Internal Revenue Code that affords its tax-favorable status.
3. Home page for ACORD, World Wide Web: http//www.acord.org
4. George L. Head and Stephen Horn, II, *Essentials of Risk Management*, 3d ed., vol. 1 (Malvern, PA: Insurance Institute of America, 1997), pp. 4-5.
5. Arthur Larson, *Workmen's Compensation for Occupational Injuries and Death*, Desk Edition (New York: Matthew Bender & Company, 1995).
6. Kansas Division of Workers Compensation, *Kansas Workmen's Compensation Carriers' and Self-Insurers' Information Letter*, March 1979.
7. Young v. Demos, 28 S.E. 891 (Ga.).
8. Larson, refer to §43.10.
9. The NAICS Web site has a tool to relate NAICS codes to SIC codes and vice versa.

Chapter 3

Underwriting Information

As discussed in Chapter 1, the underwriting decision-making process entails the following types of decisions:

1. Acceptance or rejection of the submission
2. Selection of policy provisions
3. Setting the rate
4. Whether to modify the risk through loss control
5. Whether to modify the insured's retention

Having the right information about the applicant is essential to making proper underwriting decisions. Gathering and evaluating underwriting information may uncover issues that require yet additional information before an underwriter can make the necessary decision. This does not mean that underwriters should gather as much information as possible before making a decision. Several factors limit the amount of information that the underwriter can and should collect. The challenge for the underwriter is to discern what and how much information is necessary.

This chapter describes the types of information that underwriters normally need in order to make decisions and how this information is relevant to the underwriting decision-making process. Underwriters sometimes put off making a decision on an account by requesting additional information. It is helpful for underwriters to make a distinction between information that is essential to their decisions and information that is not. The primary sources of underwriting information are the agent or broker and the application. Other sources of underwriting information are available at a cost of time and money.

Determining How Much Information To Gather

Underwriters do not have the luxury of unlimited time to gather information. They have to make decisions on a timely basis so that an applicant knows whether the insurer will provide insurance. The portion of the total premium available for evaluating an account is also limited. These two limitations require underwriters to gather information selectively. Following the guidelines established by underwriting management, underwriters must ensure that each piece of information is necessary and that the cost of each piece of information does not exceed the value it contributes to the decision-making process. This concept was defined in Chapter 1 as "information efficiency."

Categorizing Information

Underwriters sometimes use the following categories intuitively or consciously when determining whether the additional information should be obtained.

- *Essential information*—information that is absolutely necessary to arrive at the decision
- *Desirable information*—information that is not absolutely necessary but would be helpful in evaluating the account if the information can be obtained at an acceptable cost and without any undue delay
- *Available information*—information that may or may not be helpful and is not worth making any special effort to obtain

Essential information for an underwriting decision is usually specified in the insurer's underwriting guidelines. Most of the information that is requested on the commercial application would be considered essential. As most underwriters know, however, agents and brokers often do not complete the application entirely. Underwriters must then decide how much information beyond what is required to classify and rate the information is truly essential and worth the time required to obtain it. Underwriting audits are often used to determine whether information considered essential to make a sound underwriting decision is being obtained. For some insurers, essential underwriting information might be the information that, if absent, would result in the underwriter's being criticized following an underwriting audit.

What constitutes desirable and available information is usually less defined than information considered essential. Information obtained from a physical inspection of the insured's operation might be considered desirable information. If, however, the underwriter has specific concerns about a process or materials the insured uses, the physical inspection might be considered essential. An underwriter's information requirements will likely vary based on the line of business, the classification, and the underwriter's experience level. Underwriters often have a great deal of *available* information, but not all this information is relevant to the underwriting decision. The Internet, for example, has enabled underwriters to search the World Wide Web for references to the insured. In many instances, accounts maintain Web sites that provide a description of the business and the types of work they do. When available, this information serves to broaden the underwriter's understanding of the account and confirm information already obtained.

Categorizing information as essential, desirable, or available is just one approach some underwriters use to guide their decision to follow up on missing information or to request additional information. Many insurers have dollar amount thresholds that the account's premium must exceed before any inspection report can be ordered. Underwriters operating under these constraints might, for example, seek only essential information on a minimum premium account but attempt to confirm the information received with a quick Internet search. Underwriting guidelines usually provide direction to the underwriter as to how insurer resources should be used to gather information.

Balancing Account-Specific Information With General Information

Much of the information that underwriters gather is specific to the account being underwritten—its hazards, exposures, operations, and employees. Some of the information is more general. *Best's Underwriting Guide* and government statistics on the hazardous nature of various products, for example, give underwriters general information about the applicant's industry and product line, not about the applicant's specific operations or products. Although underwriters are primarily concerned with information specific to the account being underwritten, they should not ignore more general information. It helps put the account-specific information in context.

The more general information is especially helpful when underwriting an account in an industry with which the underwriter has little experience. When the underwriter has some leeway in the pricing of the account, these more general types of information can help establish a range of possible prices or determine comparable accounts for which a price has already been established.

Underwriters need to be prepared to explain the overall desirability of a class or type of account to an agent, a broker, or an applicant. If, for example, a producer calls an underwriter to ask about workers compensation insurance on a plastics manufacturer, the underwriter should be able to explain the hazards of such an account and whether the insurer would be willing to write it. The general sources, together with the insurer's underwriting guide, give the underwriter the background necessary to answer the producer's questions. Once the producer submits the account to the underwriter, the underwriter consults the more account-specific sources of information.

Initial Sources of Underwriting Information

Because underwriters must gather and process information efficiently, they should make the best possible use of the information immediately available. Two sources of information are available as soon as the underwriter receives a submission: the agent or broker and the application.

The Agent or Broker

Underwriters rely more on the agent or broker than any other person for information about the account. The agent or broker is the first person to interview the prospective client, see the property or operations to be insured, and evaluate the account's exposure to loss.

The agent or broker even has the initial option of forgoing any attempt to find an insurer to provide coverage. In some instances, agents or brokers might not be willing to handle an account because they have no experience with the particular type of account or do not represent an insurer that can handle that type of account. By making this initial decision not to proceed, the producer saves the underwriter time. As mentioned in Chapter 1, pre-screening of applicants by the agent or broker is referred to as front-line underwriting.

With first-hand knowledge of the account, the agent or broker can answer many questions for the underwriter. Agents and brokers who work frequently with an underwriter are often able to anticipate information needs and satisfy them so the underwriting decision can be expedited.

Even if the agent or broker tries to include as much information as possible with the submission, other questions arise during the initial underwriting of an account and after the account has been written. Often, an underwriter can get the answers to these questions through a phone call to the agent or broker.

The time the agent or broker spends with the applicant is important. The extent of the producer's familiarity with the prospect influences the credibility of the information on the application. Agents or brokers dealing with an account for the first time might rely heavily on statements made by the applicant. Usually agents or brokers record and communicate the information provided by the applicant without any verification other than the agent's or broker's first-hand knowledge of the account. As the agent or broker becomes more familiar with the account, the information provided by the insured can be better evaluated for completeness and accuracy.

The importance of the agent or broker to the underwriter cannot be overemphasized. The agent or broker is the primary source of dependable information. The agent or broker and the underwriter should develop a close working relationship so that each understands what the other expects and each feels free to call on the other for help. Agents and brokers should clearly understand the type of accounts the insurer prefers to write, as well as the insurer's guidelines. By working with agents and brokers on a day-to-day basis, underwriters can strengthen this working relationship.

The Application

The **application** provides information obtained directly from the applicant with the assistance of the agent or broker. Information provided by the application is expected to be truthful and complete. By signing the application, the applicant acknowledges that the statements are being relied on for underwriting and claim handling purposes. If the insured provides materially false information or conceals material information, the insured could be subject to criminal and civil penalties.

Although the style and format of the application vary among insurers, most include the same general questions. ACORD has achieved some uniformity by producing standardized applications that are used by a number of different insurers. ACORD commercial applications follow the same modular approach insurers use in providing coverage. The Commercial Insurance Application— Application Information Section (ACORD 125) is completed for all accounts. Other, coverage-specific applications are completed for each line of business the insured wants to purchase.

The application captures the name and address of the individual or organization that wants to buy insurance and the types and amounts of insurance desired. A properly completed application also provides the information needed to classify the account for rating purposes and to determine the premium. In addition, the application contains information that the underwriter needs to evaluate the submission. Depending on the type of insurance, the application might contain all the information needed. Many types of insurance, however, require a supplemental application to provide additional information. Insurers have developed supplemental applications for a variety of special purposes. These might include a particular line of business (such as directors and officers liability), a classification (such as restaurants), or an industry (such as construction trades). The term **submission** refers to the application and any other supporting information, such as product brochures, financial statements, photos, medical statements, and other materials supporting the application.

ACORD Supplemental Applications

ACORD has developed many supplemental applications that can be used for certain coverages or classes of business. Examples of these supplementary applications include the following:

- Supplemental Property Application (ACORD 190)
- Restaurant/Tavern Supplement (ACORD 185)
- Contractors Supplement (ACORD 186)
- Truckers/Motor Carriers Supplement, Request for State/Federal Filing Action (ACORD 194)

For most accounts, the information provided on the application is sufficient to make an underwriting decision. However, an underwriter might want additional information for any of the following four reasons:

- To collect missing information
- To investigate conflicting information
- To verify the accuracy of the information provided
- To handle complex accounts or ones that present a relatively high degree of risk

Most insurers have specific rules for handling missing information. The time and effort an underwriter is willing to put into obtaining it will depend on its importance. For example, if the application does not show the limits of insurance, underwriters will suspend the underwriting process until they receive that information. In other circumstances, if the name and policy number of the previous insurer are missing, the underwriter might continue to process the application while awaiting that information.

One of the most difficult challenges for an underwriter is interpreting the information on the application. Are all the applicant's answers accurate? Has the applicant revealed all the relevant information? Do the answers taken as a whole make sense? Are the applicant's answers consistent, or does one contradict another?

Some applicants try to defraud the insurance company by willfully concealing important information or by misrepresenting the facts. Fraud is a serious and expensive problem facing not only insurance companies but also the insurance-buying public. Insurance rates assume that each insured makes a fair contribution to the pool from which the many pay the losses of a few. Misleading statements on the application might lead to a lower rate than the exposure justifies. The insured benefits at the expense of other policyholders and receives an unjust reward for the deceit.

Applicants for insurance try to make themselves look as desirable as possible to the underwriter. In addition, the application might not be completely accurate because applicants simply make mistakes and misinterpret questions. Underwriters should, therefore, use other sources of information to get a more complete and accurate picture of the account. Procedures for verifying the information on the application against other sources vary from one insurer to another. Other sources of information, described in this chapter, can verify and supplement the information on the application.

The applicant's loss history and prior insurance are two of the most significant items of underwriting information on the application. Taken together, these items of information provide a composite record of the account's profitability from the perspective of its past insurers.

Loss History

Loss history is a listing of past claims, including the date of occurrence, the line of business, the type or description of the claim, the date of the claim, the amount paid, the amount reserved, and the claim's current status. The loss history section of the ACORD Commercial Insurance Application is shown in Exhibit 3-1. Loss history is one of the most important items of information an underwriter obtains about an account because past losses are a good indication of the types of losses that the account will present in the future.

Almost every insurance application contains a section asking the applicant to describe losses over a certain period of time. Large accounts often include a separate summary of losses (or loss runs) rather than a listing of losses on the application itself.

The number of years of loss experience requested varies by insurer, by class, and by line of business. Five years' worth of experience are usually requested on the application. In lines of business in which loss experience is more volatile, such as medical malpractice insurance, insurers might request more years of loss history. This longer experience period for these lines of business gives a more credible picture of the applicant's loss history. Some experienced rating plans, described in Chapter 5, require three years' worth of loss experience, not including the current year, to price specific coverages.

Exhibit 3-1
ACORD Commercial Insurance Application

LOSS HISTORY

Enter All Claims (Regardless of Fault) or Occurrences That May Give Rise To Claims for the Prior 5 Years				Check Here If None		See Attached Summary	
Date of Occurrence	Line	Type/Description of Occurrence or Claim	Date of Claim	Amount Paid	Amount Reserved	Claim	Status
9/15/XX	WC	Employee cut hand while slicing meat	9/15/XX		$1,000	X	Open
							Closed
12/1/XX	WC	Employee fell off ladder while setting up Christmas display	12/1/XX		$5,000	X	Open
							Closed

Copyright ACORD, 1993; used with permission.

Underwriters expect applicants to have had some losses. The extent to which losses are expected, however, depends on the coverage and exposures presented. An applicant for commercial auto coverage with one auto and one driver might have had five consecutive years without losses. However, an underwriter would probably not expect a loss-free history from an applicant with a large number of autos.

Because losses are expected to some degree, having them does not necessarily make an applicant unacceptable. The challenge facing the underwriter is to determine whether the account has had *too many* losses, or one suspicious or severe loss that, by its nature, causes the underwriter to question the desirability of the account. Through experience and by reviewing underwriting guidelines, underwriters develop a sense for the level of losses that are acceptable.

Underwriters usually look for trends in losses. Have the applicant's losses been increasing, decreasing, or remaining stable? That trend usually gives the underwriter an idea of what to expect. If there is only one loss, as is often the case for small commercial accounts, there is no trend at all. In this case, the underwriter analyzes when and why the loss occurred and whether the insured has taken appropriate remedial action.

The underwriter also examines loss frequency and severity. **Frequency** refers to the number of losses over a particular period. **Severity** refers to the dollar size of the losses that have occurred. Although both are important, frequency is usually a better indicator of future loss experience. Severity of the loss is often beyond the insured's control, but frequency is usually controllable.

In evaluating an applicant's loss history, the underwriter should consider the coverage the insured purchased under a prior policy. If, for example, the insured had a $1,000 deductible on the prior policy, then the loss history will likely not reflect losses the insured absorbed through the deductible. In some instances, the insured may not have purchased a particular coverage in the past—so the insured's indication that there were "no past losses" might not be helpful in using past losses to assess the likelihood of future losses.

Underwriters often have to evaluate applications in which the loss history information is left blank or for which there is the notation that loss information will follow. Most underwriters recognize that the applications they receive are being submitted to several insurers simultaneously. In a competitive insurance market, agents and brokers are likely to submit as little information as possible, particularly if it might be negative. Underwriters must often review the application based on the merits of the information presented. If the account is otherwise acceptable, the underwriter will contact the agent or broker to determine whether the insured's loss history is such that it will change his or her opinion of the account.

Prior Insurance

The ACORD application specifically asks the insured whether coverage has been declined, canceled, or nonrenewed during the past three years. If the answer is "yes," then the underwriter needs to determine whether the reason for the affirmative answer is relevant to the current underwriting decision. An insurer, for example, might decide to withdraw from a state. One approach insurers take to discontinue operations is not to offer renewals to insureds included in this book of business. However, if the applicant had been canceled or nonrenewed because of too many losses, nonpayment of premium, or an unwillingness to implement loss control recommendations, these are circumstances that would affect the desirability of the current application for insurance. Some states do not permit an insurer to ask about the disposition of prior insurance, while others prohibit the insurer from denying coverage solely because coverage was declined, canceled, or nonrenewed by another insurer.

The name of each prior insurer and policy number are usually requested on the application along with a sketch of prior coverage, premium paid, and policy expiration date. If the account is experience rated, the underwriter might have to contact the prior carrier to confirm or update the loss history provided by the insured. Additionally, underwriters are usually aware of the types of accounts that most insurers actively write. An underwriter might have additional questions for the agent or broker if the account is moving from a specialty-market insurer to a standard-market insurer, and vice versa. Underwriters can review the coverage summary to determine whether requested coverage is similar to the account's prior coverage. Why, for example, is the account requesting significantly higher (or lower) property coverage limits, or why was there no coverage before for an exposure but now coverage is requested? If the application shows the premium paid to the prior insurer, the underwriter can determine whether the insurer's quote is competitive with the account's renewal pricing. If there is a significant difference in pricing between the insurer's quote and the prior insurer's premium, the underwriter might question the accuracy of the information provided on the application.

Some applications are submitted with a proposed effective date that does not give the underwriter sufficient time to thoroughly evaluate an account. Agents and brokers often submit applications to several insurers ninety days before expiration so the insured can review the available coverage options and premium quotations. An application dated close to the expiration date usually indicates that the agent or broker has already bound coverage for the insured, so any investigation must be expedited. In this instance, a decision to not write the account will mean that the underwriter will have to issue a notice of cancellation to the insured and others who have been assured that this account has been insured by issuance of certificates of insurance. Additionally, the insurer will be responsible for insured losses while the policy is bound but before the policy is legally canceled.

Additional Sources of Underwriting Information

Many underwriting decisions are made on the basis of the application alone or on the basis of the application plus telephone conversations with the agent or broker. The underwriter can usually determine from the information presented on the application whether the account is acceptable, based on the insurer's underwriting guidelines. When underwriters have doubts about the acceptability of an account, they might be able to obtain additional information about the account from any of the following sources:

- Loss control reports

- Publications of insurance advisory organizations
- Prior insurers
- Others working for the same insurer
- Insurer files
- Financial reporting services
- Government records
- Valuation guides
- Background resource publications

Because of time and expense limitations and in some cases low premium levels, an underwriter cannot justify using every available source of information about every submission. Knowing what sources are available enables the underwriter to choose those sources that provide the necessary information most efficiently.

Loss Control Reports

When underwriters want someone other than the agent or broker submitting the application to make a physical inspection of an account, they usually request a loss control report. A **loss control report** contains information gathered specifically at the request of the underwriter by an insurer representative who visits the account and makes a report of his or her findings. The individual who conducts the visit and makes the report is usually a loss control representative.

There is no standard format for loss control reports. Many insurer-developed report formats have evolved as frequently requested information was added to the report format. Loss control reports for many insurers are a collection of separate questionnaires that are specific to each line of business being written. In addition to the standard questions that appear on loss control report forms, loss control representatives usually add a narrative description of the account. Included in this narrative are specific suggestions and recommendations that might improve the underwriting profitability of the account. Many underwriters submit the suggestions and recommendations to the agent or broker with the expectation that the insured will implement them. If the loss control report identifies a significant exposure to loss, the underwriter might insist that the loss control recommendation be implemented if coverage is to continue.

The information obtained through loss control reports, while useful, is usually expensive. Underwriting management usually establishes guidelines for underwriters that encourage them to order loss control reports on a selective basis.

One approach is not to request loss control reports on accounts that develop less than a specific dollar amount of premium.

Another approach to controlling the cost of using loss control reports is to purchase the services of an independent contractor who specializes in loss control work. These specialists are often referred to as **fee for service companies**. Fee for service companies usually have many insurers as customers and can provide loss control reports at a reasonable cost relative to what an insurer would pay for an employee to develop the information. Because of the volume of loss control reports produced, it is economically sound for fee for service companies to have representatives in many locations. The speed at which many fee for service companies can respond to requests to inspect properties is a primary benefit for insurers who use their services. A drawback of using fee for service companies is that the loss control reports they develop are usually presented in a generic format that may not meet the underwriting needs of the insurer. Fee for service companies are often willing to use insurer-developed forms, but at an additional cost.

Another cost of loss control reports is time—time that the underwriter might not have. Statutes in many states limit an insurer's right to cancel after the first sixty days of the policy's inception. After that time, cancellation may be limited to reasons such as fraud and nonpayment of premium. In most cases, however, the insurer could endorse a policy to correct improper rating based on information gathered on a loss control report, whenever found.

Because of the importance of making a quick decision on a new submission and the time required to obtain loss control reports, underwriters sometimes approve a submission subject to a favorable loss control report and subject to compliance with all loss control recommendations. In this way, underwriters can clarify to the agent or broker and the applicant that they expect a favorable report and the applicant's cooperation in correcting any problems. Receiving the loss control report quickly is still important because of the cancellation laws of many states.

Publications of Insurance Advisory Organizations

As mentioned in Chapter 1, many insurers are members of or subscribers to insurance advisory organizations. In addition to other services they provide, insurance advisory organizations produce many publications used by underwriters. These publications include rating manuals, circulars, form manuals, and classification guides.

Since the rating manuals contain the rating classifications and the rating rules, they are the primary source of information used by underwriters to classify and rate accounts properly. Because the rules in the rating manuals limit underwriters' flexibility in making decisions, underwriters constantly refer to the manuals to develop alternatives.

Rarely does the information from the rating manual help the underwriter make risk-selection decisions. Rating manuals do, however, identify attributes that make a difference in the price charged the insured. Underwriters usually focus on these attributes since they have proven to be a factor that affects the likelihood of loss or damage. For example, commercial property account pricing usually requires that the underwriter determine the construction category for the structures insured. Continuing the example, frame structures are more susceptible to loss than are noncombustible structures and therefore are more expensive to insure.

In addition, when insurance advisory organizations change rules, classifications, or loss costs, they issue circulars explaining the changes. The insurance advisory organizations design policy forms and endorsements for use with each rating plan and publish information about how to use them. Insurers often adopt the forms designed by the insurance advisory organizations.

In addition to promulgating rates and issuing rating manuals, insurance advisory organizations publish a number of guides for use by underwriters. These publications explain specific rating plans in more detail and give some background information on these plans. They also explore current topics of interest in detail. For example, the National Council on Compensation Insurance (NCCI) publishes a manual called *Scopes of Basic Manual Classifications* to assist underwriters in properly classifying accounts for workers compensation insurance. The NCCI also publishes a workers compensation experience rating plan.

Insurance advisory organizations also develop studies on important insurance industry concerns. ISO, for example, has an insurance issues series on such topic as *The Impact of Catastrophes on Property Insurance* and *Catastrophes: Insurance Issues Surrounding the Northridge Earthquake and Other Natural Disasters*. While most of these studies are aimed at underwriting management, individual underwriters will often benefit from understanding the broader issues facing insurers.

Prior Insurers

Underwriters often want loss information that can be obtained only from the prior insurer with the help of the applicant. The prior insurer is usually willing to provide loss information to others but only with the written consent of the insured.

Loss information from the prior insurer is used to confirm or supplement information provided on the application. The loss information provided by the applicant is often merely the applicant's best recollection of amounts paid by the insurer and, in many cases, the applicant may not know how much the insurer actually paid. Rather than providing misinformation, applications often indicate that loss information will be provided at a later date. If the insured does provide a loss history on the application and it does not match the information obtained from the prior insurer, the underwriter should follow up with the agent or broker to clarify discrepancies.

Loss information from the prior insurer might not always be particularly helpful. Many insurer information systems use codes or brief text messages to describe losses. A loss history generated from such a system, often referred to as a loss run, might be incomprehensible without a key to insurer loss codes.

Insurers usually do not provide much information to others beyond objective loss information such as that requested on the ACORD Commercial Insurance Application. Insurer loss files often contain subjective or confidential information about the insured that should not be shared with others.

Others Working for the Same Insurer

In addition to loss control personnel, other employees within the insurance company can aid in the information-gathering process. This group includes other underwriters, claim representatives, marketing representatives, and premium auditors. Those employees are often directly involved with the insured and can aid in verifying exiting information and developing needed information.

Other Underwriters

Underwriters within the same company can be a valuable source of information for all types of insurance. Even if they cannot help with information regarding the specific account, they might have previous experience with similar accounts, or they might be able to suggest where to look for additional information.

Claim Representatives

In the process of settling a claim, claim representatives often learn a great deal about an account, some of which might be of value to the account's underwriter. For example, in response to an auto accident, the claim representative might discover a regular operator not shown on the commercial auto application. Additionally, the claim representative is able to provide information on the condition of the insured's premises and aspects of the insured's operations that were otherwise unknown.

Even when the claim does not produce negative information about the account, underwriters often review the claim file, with its narrative and photos, to learn more about the account. Because claim representatives have proven to be such a valuable source of account information, many insurers have formalized the underwriter referral process by creating forms for just this purpose. In this way, claim representatives are likely to notify underwriters of information that they have gained first hand about an account. An example of a claim referral form is shown in Exhibit 3-2.

Marketing Representatives

Most insurers have personnel called marketing representatives, whose primary responsibility is maintaining relations with agents and brokers. This responsibility includes appointing agents, training producers in insurer policies and procedures, and establishing goals for the producer. Because marketing representatives are usually assigned a specific territory, they are familiar with that territory and many of the accounts in it. Marketing representatives sometimes help underwrite small commercial accounts when the expertise of a loss control representative is not necessary. For example, a marketing representative could easily answer an underwriter's nontechnical questions about the kinds of buildings located near the applicant's building, the condition of the parking lot, and the location of fire hydrants.

Premium Auditors

Premiums for many commercial policies are subject to an audit. This means that the premium paid at policy inception is an estimated premium and that the final premium is not determined until after the policy period has ended. For example, workers compensation premiums are based on remuneration (payroll). Because no one can predict the exact payroll for the upcoming year, the insured estimates the annual payroll and pays a premium based on that estimate. At the end of the policy period, the premium auditor examines the insured's accounting records to determine the actual payroll. If the actual payroll differs from the estimate, the insured either pays an additional premium or receives a return premium.

Premium auditors can also observe the insured's premises and operations. Because they work with the insured's financial records, auditors are in a better position than claim adjusters to comment on the insured's financial condition.

In addition, as a result of reviewing the insured's records from one year to the next, the auditor can observe changes in operations and plans for the future. These affect the underwriting desirability of the account and might be factors of which the underwriter is unaware.

Exhibit 3-2
Claim Referral Form

CLAIM REPORT TO UNDERWRITER

CONFIDENTIAL—FOR INTERNAL USE ONLY

Adjuster—Use this form when accident frequency, loss cost, conditions, or type of risk should be brought to the attention of the underwriter

DATE OF ACCIDENT/LOSS	INCURRED COST OR RESERVE		CLAIM NUMBER	
9/1/2000	$50,000		CGL 8675309	

	PRODUCING BRANCH OFFICE	UNDERWRITING DEPARTMENT	CAUSE CODE	POLICY NUMBER	INCEPTION	EXPIRATION
TO:	Elliott Arnold		721	CGL 1239871	7/1/2000	7/1/2001

FROM:	CLAIM OFFICE	LIMITS	PRODUCING AGENT	CO.	BRANCH OFFICE	AGENCY CODE
	Harrisburg, PA	$2 million	L. Brandon	IIA	Malvern	1201

INSURED'S NAME	INSURED'S MAILING ADDRESS (STREET)		CITY	STATE	ZIP CODE
Gravel Hauling, Inc.	701 Sugartown Road		Malvern	PA	19355

LOCATION OF ACCIDENT/PREMISES INVOLVED (STREET ADDRESS)			CITY	STATE	ZIP CODE
Hwy 30—East of Lancaster, PA			Gap	PA	19387

FULL NAME OF DRIVER OF INSURED VEHICLE (AUTO OR MOTOR TRUCK CARGO) *OR* INJURED EMPLOYEE (WORKERS COMP.)

Insured driver, John Jennings, rear-ended a stopped school bus. Only seven school children and the driver were on the bus at the time.

☑ **ANY ACTION DEEMED NECESSARY WILL NOT AFFECT THE DISPOSITION OF THIS CLAIM.**
☐ **ANY ACTION DEEMED NECESSARY MAY AFFECT THE DISPOSITION OF THIS CLAIM.**

INSTRUCTIONS TO ADJUSTER: Check applicable blocks below and explain each item checked under REMARKS.

A. AUTOMOBILE

- ☐ 1. Physical disability
- ☐ 2. Vehicle in poor condition
- ☐ 3. Evidence of drinking
- ☐ 4. Reckless driving
- ☐ 5. Uncooperative
- ☐ 6. Loss frequency
- ☐ 7. Poor driving record
- ☐ 8. Driver under age 25*
- ☐ 9. Indiscriminate loan of vehicle
- ☐ 10. Driver fell asleep
- ☑ 11. Gross negligence
- ☐ 12. Total loss of insured vehicle
- ☐ 13. Late notice
- ☐ 14. Owned vehicle not on policy
- ☐ 15. Other

*Personal auto policy not so classified

B. WORKERS COMPENSATION OR GENERAL LIABILITY

- ☐ 1. Hazardous physical condition
- ☐ 2. Machinery
- ☐   a. Defectively manufactured
- ☐   b. Poorly designed
- ☐   c. Does not meet industry norm standards
- ☐   d. Inadequately labeled
- ☐ 3. Poor location
- ☐ 4. Uncooperative
- ☐ 5. Poor management or supervision
- ☐ 6. Inadequate records
- ☐ 7. Loss frequency
- ☐ 8. Late notice
- ☐ 9. Pollution loss
- ☐ 10. Other

C. FIDELITY, OR BURGLARY, OR PLATE GLASS, OR FIRE MARINE AND MULTI-LINE

- ☐ 1. Indadequate safeguards or training
- ☐ 2. Inadequate records
- ☐ 3. Loss frequency
- ☐ 4. Possible illegal activities
- ☐ 5. Questionable loss
- ☐ 6. Vacant premises
- ☐ 7. Underinsured
- ☐ 8. Questionable physical condition
- ☐ 9. Late notice
- ☐ 10. Poor housekeeping
- ☐ 11. Uncooperative
- ☐ 12. Possible financial problems
- ☐ 13. Exposure from adjoining risks
- ☐ 14. Fire protection/first aid system impeded
- ☐ 15. Carelessness
- ☐ 16. Other

REMARKS   Driver should have had an unobstructed view of the stopped school bus. The bus's flashing lights were working and in use. Long work hours at the quarry might have contributed to the driver's lack of attention.

ADJUSTER'S SIGNATURE K. Harrington | **C.R.U. DATE** 9/2/2000

The auditor's report shows the proper classifications and payroll amounts and thus serves as a check on the initial classification and payroll estimates made at policy inception. If the insured is involved in operations not shown on the policy, they will appear on the copy of the audit billing sent to the underwriter. This may indicate a need to endorse the current policy to reflect an additional classification or higher payroll.

Finally, the premium auditor can also be a source of information during the selection portion of the decision-making process. Drawing on the premium auditor's in-depth knowledge of rating and classification procedures before policy issuance might prevent classification (and premium collection) problems after the policy has expired. Underwriters should contact premium auditors with questions about classifications. Some insurers send a premium auditor to visit an insured's premises at the beginning of the policy year to ascertain that the insured understands what records are required and how they should be kept. In a few instances, some of the insured's operations may call for a separate classification and rate. If the insured keeps the proper records, the premiums will reflect the exposure more accurately and disputes about the audit will be less likely.

Exhibit 3-3 is a sample of a form used by auditors to report significant information to the underwriting department. Exhibit 3-4 is the form that the underwriter would then use to report the action taken, if any.

Insurer Files

When the underwriter receives a submission for new business, the insurer might already have some information or even an entire file on the account. That information can often help in the underwriting evaluation. The ability of the underwriter to locate the information depends on the insurer's record-keeping and file-retention practices.

Accounts Declined, or Accounts Quoted and Not Written

Most insurers have some system for keeping previous applications for which the insurer declined to write insurance or for which the applicant did not accept the quote. These files can be valuable in evaluating new business. Because they document earlier decisions, they can greatly reduce the amount of work that a new application requires.

If an account was previously declined, the underwriter can focus on the reasons for the decision and changes since that might now make the account desirable. Otherwise, the account should probably be declined again. By focusing only on the reasons for the previous declination, the underwriter can spend less time gathering the information a decision requires.

Exhibit 3-3
Premium Audit Notice to Underwriting

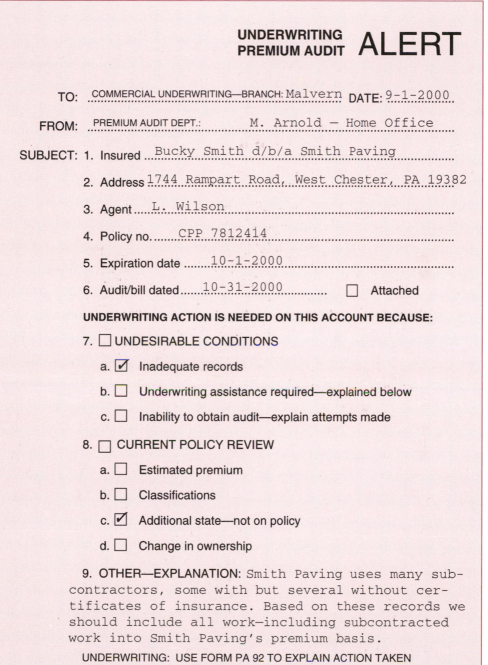

UNDERWRITING
PREMIUM AUDIT **ALERT**

TO: COMMERCIAL UNDERWRITING—BRANCH: Malvern   DATE: 9-1-2000

FROM: PREMIUM AUDIT DEPT.:   M. Arnold — Home Office

SUBJECT: 1. Insured Bucky Smith d/b/a Smith Paving

2. Address 1744 Rampart Road, West Chester, PA 19382

3. Agent L. Wilson

4. Policy no. CPP 7812414

5. Expiration date 10-1-2000

6. Audit/bill dated 10-31-2000   ☐ Attached

UNDERWRITING ACTION IS NEEDED ON THIS ACCOUNT BECAUSE:

7. ☐ UNDESIRABLE CONDITIONS

   a. ☑ Inadequate records

   b. ☐ Underwriting assistance required—explained below

   c. ☐ Inability to obtain audit—explain attempts made

8. ☐ CURRENT POLICY REVIEW

   a. ☐ Estimated premium

   b. ☐ Classifications

   c. ☑ Additional state—not on policy

   d. ☐ Change in ownership

9. **OTHER—EXPLANATION:** Smith Paving uses many sub-contractors, some with but several without certificates of insurance. Based on these records we should include all work—including subcontracted work into Smith Paving's premium basis.

UNDERWRITING: USE FORM PA 92 TO EXPLAIN ACTION TAKEN
AS A RESULT OF THIS ALERT.

Exhibit 3-4

Underwriting Responses to Premium Audit Alert

UNDERWRITING RESPONSE TO AUDIT ALERT

TO: Premium Audit Department

FROM: Commercial Underwriting: E. Albright

RE: Insured: Bucky Smith d/b/a Smith Paving

         Policy Number: CPP 7812414   Expiration Date: 10-1-2000

☑ Renewal policy **has** been endorsed to
increase premium basis in accordance with
final audit. *(Need Underwriting Approval
Stamp only.)*

Underwriting Stamp
E A—U/W 11-3-2000

☐ Other action requested has been taken.
(Need Underwriting Approval Stamp only.)

☑ The following action has been taken.
(Need Underwriting Approval Stamp only.)

 Informed L. Wilson that we
would revise the audit if the
Smith Paving CPA put records in
better order.

☐ No action taken. *(Need General Manager
Stamp only.)*
Reason: _____

_____

_____

_____

General Manager Stamp

Form PA 92

Accounts Previously Insured

Insurers keep records on accounts previously insured for a number of legal reasons. Underwriting information, however, is usually stripped from the paper file within a year of two of the date that the policy was canceled or nonrenewed. If that account is resubmitted before underwriting information is removed, the underwriter will have the benefit of information obtained previously. Even if the underwriting information is gone—and it would likely be useless if it were too old—the underwriter would probably have access to some policy information captured in the insurer's information system.

Files for Other Coverages

In some cases, an insurer might already provide some coverage for the applicant. For example, an account that has auto coverage with the insurer might apply for property coverage. The file for the auto coverage might help the property underwriter. If the auto underwriter recently analyzed the insured's financial condition, the property underwriter need only refer to that analysis.

Loss control reports can also be helpful, even if they were completed for another line of insurance. Assume, for example, that the auto loss control report indicates that the insured is safety conscious, carefully maintains its vehicles, and replaces vehicles at regular intervals. The property underwriter could infer that the insured would care for the machinery and equipment covered by property insurance in the same way. Depending on the coverages, limits, and date of the auto report, the property underwriter might decide that a new loss control report is not necessary.

Finally, the loss history of the coverage already written might reveal important information for underwriting the new coverage. Perhaps the claim representative has noted significant factors regarding the insured. For example, the current business might be scheduled to be nonrenewed, and the insurer might not want additional business from this insured.

Financial Reporting Services

Financial data are an important source of information in determining the desirability of an account. Financial analysis involves the comparison, interpretation, and evaluation of financial data. Major sources of financial data include the financial statements of companies and reports from financial reporting services. With the help of financial and credit analyses, experienced underwriters can assess various types of data as indicators of the following:

- Moral and morale hazards
- Policyholders' ability to pay premiums
- A company's financial strength and soundness of management

Financial statements are the starting point in the evaluation of the financial health of an account. Most underwriters do not possess sophisticated financial analysis skills. In certain lines of business, notably surety bonds, the underwriter must be a skilled financial analyst. In most other lines of insurance an underwriter needs to understand the results of financial analysis but does not need to be proficient in performing the analysis itself. The information provided by financial reporting service companies will meet most, if not all, of an underwriter's needs.

Financial reporting services perform financial analysis and prepare reports to meet a variety of insurance company needs. Although most of these reports are not designed for financial experts, an underwriter does need to know the basics of financial analysis in order to use them effectively. Chapter 4 examines the basics of financial analysis.

Several organizations collect, analyze, and disseminate financial and operational data on businesses. These firms include Dun & Bradstreet,[1] Experian,[2] Central Analysis Bureau,[3] and Equifax.[4] The largest is Dun & Bradstreet (D&B), which provides reports geared to the needs of businesses that extend credit to a wide range of businesses. Experian and Equifax offer similar services. Central Analysis Bureau, by contrast, focuses on the trucking industry and offers an analysis of filings truckers make with the United States Department of Transportation.

The business of D&B and similar organizations is gathering and maintaining information on commercial enterprises and supplying that data to legitimately interested subscribers, including underwriters. Underwriters who are faced with the continuing task of measuring the account's financial stability can benefit considerably by using these organizations. Accordingly, underwriters need to be thoroughly familiar with the services available from the various sources and able to interpret the data provided.

One of the major reasons for using financial reporting organizations is the scope of their activities. These organizations investigate and analyze thousands of commercial enterprises on a continuing basis. They typically (1) report on the history of the company and the background of its owners and managers; (2) describe, in detail, the method of operation; (3) outline the company's paying record; and (4) analyze financial status, operating results, and trends. D&B also assigns a composite credit rating.

The analytical information substantially reduces the effort necessary to analyze accounts. Since underwriting costs are largely determined by time, these outside services help underwriters investigate applications as completely and rapidly as possible. Information from outside sources also has the advantage of having come from a neutral third party, so it tends to be less subject to bias. Reporting agencies, however, must sometimes rely on data provided directly by owners of the company investigated. Although other sources can confirm much of this information, an owner's or a manager's financial estimates will obviously be less precise than an accountant's audited financial statements. Underwriters should appreciate the need for closer attention to reports and analyses based largely on the owner's representations.

Insurer underwriting guidelines are usually explicit about how underwriters should use financial reporting services. The guidelines might require that each applicant be researched using a financial reporting service database or that applicants with specific characteristics, such as businesses subject to high failure rates, be researched.

The Cost of Financial Reporting Services

In some cases, the more detailed reports can be expensive. As with any piece of underwriting information, a report must be used with discretion. An underwriting training manager might ask, "Why should I pay for a credit reporting agency to analyze the insured's financial status when I have spent quite a bit of money on training my underwriters how to read and analyze financial reports?" A credit report might be necessary to get some basic information; on the other hand, more detailed or specialized reports might be unnecessary if underwriters can make the calculations performed by the credit reporting agency. Although credit reports can be expensive, insurers purchase the reports because of the perception that the credit reporting agency's collection of financial data is thorough and its analyses are superior. Timeliness and accuracy of the reports might be given greater weight in a cost/benefit analysis of the value of using credit reports even when underwriters have the necessary expertise.

When To Order a Report

Underwriters should occasionally order a credit report after the account has been accepted and a policy issued. For example, the underwriter might be considering canceling the policy or not renewing coverage without a premium adjustment. A credit report would indicate whether any of the following conditions exist:

- Declining sales
- Debt in excess of net worth
- New management
- Operations at a loss

- Large buildup of inventory
- Slow payment record
- Insufficient working capital
- Lower rating than previous listing

Most credit-reporting agencies provide information through their Internet World Wide Web sites. Through this service, underwriters are provided almost instant access to credit information. Timely information oftentimes enables an underwriter to make a better decision.

Government Records

A variety of government records can be useful in underwriting. Motor vehicle reports are the most common example, but many others exist.

Motor Vehicle Reports

The most often used government record is the driving record of an individual seeking auto insurance. This record is usually called the motor vehicle report, or MVR.

An operator's driving record (accidents and violations) is an important predictor of future losses. MVRs are primarily used in commercial auto underwriting. In addition, MVRs are sometimes ordered if the person is operating some other type of motorized equipment, such as contractors equipment. Insurers obtain MVRs directly from a state agency or through a third-party vendor that directs the request to the state agency. Some insurers have the organization performing the inspection include an MVR as part of the inspection report.

MVRs are not perfectly accurate. Many accidents or violations never appear on an MVR for a variety of reasons. Local police or sheriff departments vary widely in their reporting of violations to the state. A driver involved in an accident not involving another vehicle might not be ticketed even though he or she clearly violated a law. Less often, violations appearing on the MVR are incorrect. That is, the MVR shows a conviction that the applicant did not receive. Finally, some states are slow in updating the records of drivers.

Many states have regulations regarding who can obtain MVRs and under what conditions they can be obtained. Some states require the insurer to have the written permission of the driver. Underwriters should know the regulations governing MVRs in their states. Regardless of the drawbacks, an MVR is the most frequently used outside source of information for auto insurance.

Other Government Records

Underwriters use a number of other government records under special circumstances. These sources include court records, real estate records, corporate filings, and government research.

Court records are sometimes helpful to an underwriter. Bankruptcy filings, pending lawsuits (both those filed *by* the applicant and those filed *against* the applicant), and records of settled lawsuits can be important sources of information. Verdicts relating to the applicant's products would be significant to a products liability underwriter. Lawsuits filed by the applicant might result in personal injury claims. Property as well as liability underwriters would be concerned if the applicant had financial difficulties and filed for bankruptcy.

Real estate records are also helpful. If the applicant has more than one mortgage outstanding on a single property, or if there are liens against the property, the applicant's financial stability might be questionable.

Publicly traded companies must file another type of government record, the 10-K, with the Securities and Exchange Commission (SEC). Most commercial accounts are not publicly traded and are therefore not required to file a 10-K. For the commercial accounts that do file them, 10-Ks are useful because they provide not only extensive financial information, but also a detailed history of the company, a description of current operations, and, possibly, plans for the future. A 10-K can be obtained directly from the applicant, from the SEC, or from an organization that specializes in obtaining 10-Ks. Information submitted to the SEC is available on the Internet.

Finally, the government collects a wealth of information on various industries, products, and organizations. This information includes (1) a ranking of industries according to the number and severity of employee injuries, (2) a ranking of products according to frequency and severity of injuries caused by the product, (3) records of employee injuries for specific organizations, and (4) product recall information.

Valuation Guides

For commercial property and inland marine insurance, the underwriter must verify the values of insured property. If the value shown on the application is too low, the underwriter will not receive sufficient premium. If the value on the application is too high, the insured will pay for coverage it does not need. In addition, if the policy limit exceeds the value of the property, the insured might be tempted to cause a loss intentionally or might not protect the property from loss, in order to collect the proceeds of insurance.

Underwriters have a number of ways to verify values the insured submits. One way involves comparing values on the submission to an outside estimate of the values. Some fee for service companies, for example, estimate building values as part of their reports. Producers often have a "value estimator" to help determine values. In many cases, these are the same tools that underwriters use. Also, underwriters can have the applicant or insured hire an appraisal company to appraise the property.

More commonly, underwriters use a valuation guidebook or computer software supplied by an appraisal company to make their own estimates. By using factors such as the age of the structure, the construction materials, the number and type of outbuildings, and the square footage of the property, underwriters can determine an estimated value. The two leading vendors of these guidebooks are American Appraisal Associates[5] and Marshall & Swift.[6] Both companies offer a variety of services, ranging from traditional valuation guides to computer software. The initial estimate in these books is adjusted to reflect any features of the property that affect its value but that are not reflected in the initial valuation. The final estimate might also reflect geographical differences in construction costs.

Underwriters use valuation guides not only for verifying building values, but also for valuing contents and machinery and equipment. An underwriter cannot possibly know the values of all the different types of machinery and equipment used by commercial enterprises.

Commercial property forms provide coverage on an actual cash value basis, but most accounts request coverage on a replacement cost basis. Underwriters need to know on which basis the value of the property was determined.

Replacement cost is simply the cost of replacing a piece of property or equipment at its current cost. If the insured has a twenty-year-old, one-story, brick warehouse of 35,000 square feet, what would it cost to build the same building today? The answer to this question would be the building's replacement cost.

Depreciation is the loss in value that develops as items age, wear out, or become obsolete. A brand new building obviously has more value than a twenty-year-old building does (assuming that the older building has had no improvements). This difference in value is the depreciation of the older building.

Actual cash value (ACV) is commonly defined as the replacement cost of the property at the time of loss, less depreciation. Over time, depreciation is deducted from the replacement cost in determining ACV; functional and economic obsolescence is also deducted. In some states, the definition of ACV considers the fair market value of the property. Depending on where the

building is located and its condition, an increase or decrease from the benchmark replacement cost less depreciation value is appropriate.

Background Resource Publications

Several additional sources of information are helpful in underwriting specific
accounts. These include a wide variety of background publications written by
experts. Some of these publications are specifically designed for use in insurance or underwriting. Some of the better known and more readily available
publications include *Best's Underwriting Guide* and *Best's Loss Control Engineering Manual* (A. M. Best Company[7]), *FC&S Bulletins* (the National Underwriter Company[8]), *Classification Guide* (Premium Audit Advisory Service[9]),
and *Commercial Liability Insurance and Commercial Property Insurance* (both
from the International Risk Management Institute[10]).

Although other publications are designed for people outside the insurance
industry, the information they contain is often helpful for evaluating accounts
from an engineering standpoint or with regard to technical subjects. Examples
include the *Fire Protection Handbook* published by the National Fire Prevention Association (NFPA)[11] and the books used by the trucking industry for
setting the retail and wholesale values for new and used trucks.

Underwriters should also have ready access to a publication that describes the
hazardous properties of chemicals and materials that businesses may use to
produce their products or provide their services.

Summary

Underwriters must determine whether they have sufficient information to
make sound underwriting decisions on an account. Many underwriters find
this determination challenging because of a natural tendency to confirm a
decision by obtaining yet one additional item of information. Such a tendency
is not practical for underwriters and their insurers. Underwriters must often
remind themselves of the concept of information efficiency in which the cost
of the information is weighed against its value in making an underwriting
decision. Some underwriters find it helpful to categorize the information they
want as being essential, desirable, or available in order to determine whether
the information should be obtained. In addition to prioritizing the information they need, underwriters seek to balance account-specific information
with general underwriting information.

The best sources of information about an account are the application and the
agent or broker who helped the insured complete it. Insurance applications are

designed to capture most, if not all, of the information needed to make an underwriting decision. However, missing and incomplete information might require the underwriter to contact the agent or broker to fill in what is not there. Also, one item of information on the application might seem to conflict with another item on the application and be a significant enough issue to resolve quickly.

Underwriters often need additional information, which can be obtained from the sources described below:

- Loss control reports provide an objective evaluation of the physical hazards of an account. They also include recommendations for controlling losses.

- Rating manuals contain the classification rules and the characteristics that distinguish one classification from another.

- Other insurance companies can confirm coverage or can provide loss runs for the account if the applicant requests them.

- Other employees—other underwriters, claim representatives, marketing representatives, and premium auditors—can be a source of additional information for a particular account.

- The insurer's files might already contain important information if the account was previously submitted or if the insurer provides other coverage for the same account.

- When the applicant's financial condition is a concern, the underwriter can request financial statements or order a report from a financial reporting service.

- Motor vehicle reports, court records, and other government records can be an important source in some situations.

- Valuation guides and various reference publications also provide a background resource for underwriters.

The multitude of sources for underwriting information poses a significant challenge for underwriters. They must constantly decide what information to use and when to use it. Gathering too much information slows down the underwriting process and drives up expenses, but having too little information can lead to bad decisions. With experience, underwriters learn to judge when they have enough information and when they need more.

Chapter Notes

1. Home page for Dun & Bradstreet, World Wide Web: http://www.dnb.com

2. Home page for Experian, World Wide Web: http://www.experian.com

3. Home page for Central Analysis Bureau, World Wide Web: http://www.cabfinancial.com

4. Home page for Equifax, World Wide Web: http://www.equifax.com

5. Home page for American Appraisal Associates, World Wide Web: http://www.american-appraisal.com

6. Home page for Marshall & Swift, World Wide Web: http://www.marshallswift.com

7. Home page for the A.M. Best Company, World Wide Web: http://www.ambest.com

8. Home page for the National Underwriter Company, World Wide Web: http://www.nuco.com

9. Home page for the Premium Audit Advisory Services (PAAS), World Wide Web: http://www.iso.com. PAAS is a subsidiary of ISO.

10. Home page for the International Risk Management Institute, World Wide Web: http://www.irmi.com

11. Home page for the National Fire Prevention Association, World Wide Web: http://www.nfpa.org

Chapter 4

Financial Analysis

Financial statements are a valuable source of information. Owners and managers use financial information in making decisions and informed judgments while planning, directing, and controlling the business. Financial information aids potential investors who want to know what the projected earnings of the business might be. Creditors want to know the creditworthiness of the business, that is, how likely it is that the business will repay its debts. Underwriters use an account's financial information to gauge its managerial competence. Financial information can also be used to determine whether moral hazard exists.

Financial reporting services, described in Chapter 3, provide an analysis of financial information. Usually, this analysis is designed to meet the specific needs of the underwriter. Many insurers choose not to use external financial reporting services and prefer that their underwriters instead perform this analysis themselves. Even those insurers that purchase external financial analysis from others often want their underwriters to know the basics of financial analysis so that they can better understand the information provided.

This chapter provides the basics of financial analysis that will be useful to underwriters who perform the analysis themselves or who review externally obtained reports. First this chapter describes the balance sheet and income statement. These are the primary sources of financial information and the source of the information used in ratio analysis, the next topic described in the chapter. Many accounts must provide more financial information than that contained in the balance sheet and income statement. Some financial statements provide insight into management's view of past events and its future business plans.

Financial Statements

Two basic financial statements are the balance sheet and the income statement. These statements are the primary sources of information for financial analysis. The ABC Corporation example, introduced in the next section, will be used to demonstrate financial analysis techniques.

The Balance Sheet

The **balance sheet** shows what is *owned* and *owed* by a firm *as of a given point in time*. The balance sheet, sometimes called the statement of financial position, is a snapshot of the organization's financial position.

The balance sheet is composed of three basic components: assets, liabilities, and owners' equity. The relationship among these categories is defined by the accounting equation.

Assets = Liabilities + Owners' equity

Assets are the properties and property rights that a business owns. These items are typically arranged on the balance sheet in descending order of liquidity. **Liabilities** represent the creditors' interests in the assets and are typically listed in order of when they become due. Owners' equity is the residual interest of the owners in the assets of the firm after creditors' interests have been satisfied. In essence, owners' equity is the difference between total assets and total liabilities. Owners' equity (or stockholders' equity in the case of a corporation) is also referred to as net worth.

There are two commonly used formats for displaying balance sheet information. The **account form** has assets listed on the left-hand side of the page, and the liabilities and stockholders' equity on the right-hand side. In the **report form**, the statement is formatted vertically so that the liabilities and stockholders' equity sections are listed below the asset section.

Any analysis of the balance sheet items should take into account one inherent limitation of the statement. Because the balance sheet represents only one moment in the life of an organization, it can be deceiving. Seasonal fluctuations, for example, might cause significant variation from the normal financial condition reported at any time. Management can also manipulate the accounts to enhance the position of a business at any point.

For example, a company can improve its current ratio (current assets divided by current liabilities) by repaying short-term debt just before the balance sheet date. The repayment of short-term debt increases the current ratio. If a company has current assets of $100,000 and current liabilities of $75,000 (before repayment), its current ratio is 1.33 ($100,000/$75,000). If the firm has $10,000 in cash available for repayment and actually does repay $10,000 of its debt, it can increase the current ratio to 1.38 ($90,000/$65,000). Although such practices (often termed "window dressing") are legal, they can be misleading, and many consider the techniques unethical.

The financial position of the ABC Company, as illustrated by the balance sheet in Exhibit 4-1, can be compared between two points in time. This analysis is accomplished through what is called a **comparative balance sheet**. A comparative balance sheet is more valuable to an analyst than a single period balance sheet because it affords the ability to look at the company's position at more than one point and compare the sets of data. Financial statements often contain a five- or ten-year summary of balance sheet data.

Comparative financial statements are created by placing two balance sheets or income statements from two different time periods side by side. Analysis of the changes from one to the other shows whether the company is gaining or losing financial strength.

Once familiar with the format and various classifications of the balance sheet, underwriters can begin to interpret the data and develop answers to a number of underwriting questions. Various tools are available to facilitate analysis of the balance sheet. For example, multiple years statements can be compared by indexing data from each statement to a common base year (a process called a trend analysis) or developing common-size statements that relate each data item as a percentage of total assets (for the balance sheet) or total sales (for the income statement).

Assets

Assets are usually divided into two major classifications: current assets and property, plant, and equipment (noncurrent assets). **Current assets** include cash and other assets that are expected to be converted into cash or used in the operation of the business within one year.

Current assets are usually listed in the order of their liquidity, as follows:

- Cash
- Marketable securities
- Receivables (accounts and notes)
- Inventories
- Prepaid expenses

Cash is always listed first and includes coins, currency, and cash equivalents such as checks, bank drafts, money orders, and demand deposits in commercial

Exhibit 4-1
ABC Company
Comparative Balance Sheet ($thousands)

Assets		
	Dec. 31, 20X5	Dec. 31, 20X4
Current Assets		
Cash	$ 40	$ 50
Marketable Securities	90	142
Prepaid Expenses	10	8
Receivables (net)	215	200
Inventories	300	350
Total Current Assets	$ 655	$ 750
Property, Plant, and Equipment		
At Cost	2,500	2,000
Less Accumulated Depreciation	650	400
Net Property, Plant, and Equipment	1,850	1,600
Total Assets	$2,505	$2,350
Liabilities and Stockholders' Equity		
	Dec. 31, 20X5	Dec 31, 20X4
Current Liabilities		
Accounts Payable	$ 80	$ 65
Notes Payable	120	100
Accruals	12	10
Provision for Federal Income Taxes	135	130
Total Current Liabilities	$ 347	$ 305
Mortgage Payable	625	650
Total Liabilities	972	955
Stockholders' Equity		
Capital Stock (100,000 shares)	1,000	1,000
Retained Earnings	533	395
Total Stockholders' Equity	1,533	1,395
Total Liabilities and Stockholders' Equity	$2,505	$2,350

banks. If cash is held for some designated purpose, such as the eventual retirement of a bond issue, it is not included as a cash item but is placed in an account designated for the specific purpose.

Marketable securities are temporary investments that can easily be converted into cash. Companies usually invest in marketable securities when they have excess funds that are not immediately needed in operations.

Receivables consist of the amounts owed to the company by customers and other outsiders. Receivables are often subdivided into notes receivable and accounts receivable.

Inventories consist of goods available for sale to customers. For a manufacturing company, the inventory item also includes two other types of inventories: raw materials and finished goods.

Prepaid expenses represent the amount that has already been paid for services that have not been received or used. A common example of a prepaid expense item is **prepaid insurance**. The ABC Company, on November 1, 20X5, paid $12,000 for an annual policy but had expended only $2,000 by December 31, 20X5 ($1,000 for each month of coverage). The remaining $10,000 is a prepaid expense.

The other major asset classification on the ABC Company's balance sheet is **property, plant, and equipment**. This category includes assets that have a useful life of more than one year, are used in the operation of the business, and are not intended for resale to customers. Examples of property, plant, and equipment are land, buildings, and an auto fleet. Land is shown on the balance sheet at its original cost. Land has an unlimited life and, therefore, is never depreciated. Buildings, machinery, and equipment, however, are valued at their original cost less an amount for accumulated depreciation. Instead of charging the entire cost of such an asset to any one year as an expense, ABC is able to spread the cost over a given number of years through the use of periodic depreciation charges. The total amount that has been expensed up to the date of the financial statement is known as **accumulated depreciation**. Financial statements reflect accounting depreciation, not *physical* depreciation. Accumulated **physical depreciation** is considered in determining the actual cash value of the asset for insurance purposes. The accounting depreciation has no direct relationship to physical depreciation.

Three other major classifications of assets might appear on balance sheets. **Investments** are listed between the current assets and property, plant, and equipment categories. These are the investments that are held for an indefinite period of time or for some designated purpose. Investment in the stocks and bonds of another company, real estate held for income-producing purposes, and investments held for a special fund such as a pension fund would all be classified as investments.

Physical and Functional Depreciation Versus Accounting Depreciation

Physical depreciation is a depreciable asset's wear and tear over a period of time. Buildings and equipment, for example, are affected by use and wear and must eventually be replaced. Functional depreciation is caused by obsolescence or inadequate performance of the asset. Many assets, for example, are affected by economic change or advancing technology and they become useless before they actually wear out. Accounting depreciation is used to spread the cost of an asset over its useful economic life. For example, an asset purchased for $100,000 with an estimated useful life of 10 years (with no residual value) could be depreciated on a straight-line basis so that $10,000 of its value depreciated annually. In its fifth year, its accounting value would be $50,000, but its market value might be $20,000 because of deterioration caused by weather. Alternatively, the market value of this asset could be negligible because a better and more efficient asset is now available.

Underwriters are concerned about the valuation of assets because property insurance policies promise to pay the actual cash value or replacement cost of the insured's property. In some instances, the insured will not understand why the insurer's approach to property valuation is different from that taken on its financial statements.

Intangible assets make up another major asset classification often found on balance sheets. These are assets that lack physical substance but have a real value to the organization. Common examples of intangible assets are patents, copyrights, franchises, and goodwill. Goodwill is reported only when a firm has been acquired or merged with another firm. The amount reported for goodwill is the excess of the price paid for the business over the book value or agreed value of all tangible net assets of the acquired firm. Accounting standards require amortization of goodwill over a period not to exceed forty years.

The last major classification of assets is known as **other assets**. These are simply those assets that cannot be otherwise classified. Items commonly found in this category are the cash surrender value of life insurance owned by the company on its officers, receivables from officers, and miscellaneous funds held for special purposes.

Liabilities

Liabilities of the company are generally found on the right-hand side of the balance sheet and are divided into two major classifications—current liabilities and noncurrent liabilities.

Current liabilities are those obligations whose payment is reasonably expected to require the use of cash or the creation of other current liabilities within one year. Current liabilities are usually listed in the probable order in which they will become due.

Examples of current liabilities include accounts payable, notes payable, the estimated amount for income taxes, and accruals. Accruals are those obligations that are owed because of the passage of time but that will be paid in the future. A common example of an accrual is accrued wages payable. If the ABC Company, on December 31, 20X5, owes its employees $12,000 for wages already earned but not payable until the following week, that $12,000 must be set up as a current liability because it is an obligation of the company.

Obligations that are due more than a year from the date of the balance sheet are listed after the total for current liabilities. Notes, bonds, and mortgages are the types of obligations considered not to be current assets.

Owners' Equity

Owners' equity, or **net worth**, represents the difference between total assets and total liabilities as of the balance sheet date. It represents the value of the owners' interest in the business. Owners' equity is reported differently for sole proprietorships, partnerships, and corporations.

The ABC Company used in the examples in this chapter is a corporation. Because the stockholders own the corporation, the net worth of ABC Company is referred to as **stockholders' equity**. Two items—capital stock and retained earnings—usually make up the stockholders' equity section.

Capital stock is the amount of funds that the stockholders have contributed through the purchase of stock. Assume that the ABC Company sold 100,000 shares of stock with a par value of $10 per share. This would account for the $1,000,000 capital stock figure. Stock often sells for more than par value. When it does, any excess over par value is reported as **additional paid-in capital** (or capital in excess of par). If the stock of ABC Company (having a par value of $10) sold for $12, it would report capital stock as being $1,000,000 and additional paid-in capital as $200,000 [($12 − $10) × 100,000].

Retained earnings are a part of the total stockholders' equity that represents the accumulated undistributed earnings of the corporation. That is, this item represents the total profits of the firm less total dividends paid and losses sustained from the date of organization. If the business operates at a net loss, retained earnings are a negative number written within parantheses.

A sole proprietorship reports owners' equity in a slightly different manner. The statement simply reports the firm's net worth as capital belonging to the owner. A partnership reports owners' equity in a similar manner.

The Income Statement

The **income statement**, once called a **profit and loss statement**, summarizes results obtained from business operations over a period of time (usually one year). This is in contrast to the balance sheet, which represents the financial position of a company at one particular time.

The income statement details the revenue and the various expenses incurred during the year. The excess of total revenue over total expenditures during this period constitutes the profit to the organization. If expenses exceed revenue, the organization incurs a loss.

Underwriters must understand and appreciate the relationship between the income statement and the balance sheet. If a net profit is realized over the course of a year, the net worth of the firm has been increased by the amount of the profit (assuming no dividends). This increase in net worth is shown on the balance sheet as an increase to retained earnings in the owners' equity section. Conversely, if the company experiences a net loss during the year, the owners' equity in the company has decreased.

The presentation of the income statement varies with the type of business. Exhibit 4-2 shows sample condensed income statements for a service business and a manufacturing firm.

The income statement illustration shown in Exhibit 4-3 is that of a merchandising firm. In ABC Company's income statement, net sales is the first entry item. **Net sales** represent the gross sales of the period less all returns and allowances. Net sales do not include any sales tax revenue.

The **cost of sales** is the second item found on the income statement. This item represents the cost to the company of merchandise sold or services provided during the year. The cost of sales is developed from the inventory at the beginning of the period adjusted for all purchases made during the period, less those goods on hand at the end of the period. When the cost of sales is subtracted from net sales, the resulting figure is the **gross margin on sales**, often referred to as the **gross profit**.

Selling, general, and administrative expenses are then subtracted from gross profit. These expenses are often referred to as operating expenses. Selling expenses include those items that can be directly related to the sales of the goods. Examples of sales expenses include such accounts as sales commissions, advertising displays, delivery expenses, and depreciation on store furniture and equipment. General and administrative expenses are those expenses that cannot be related directly to the selling of the goods but are necessary in the operation of the business. Examples include officers' and clerical salaries, office supplies used, postage fees, telephone fees, business licenses and fees, and depreciation of office furniture and fixtures. Deducting selling, general, and administrative expenses from gross margin on sales yields **operating income**. This is the income that results from the normal operations of the business during the period covered by the statement.

Exhibit 4-2
Sample Condensed Income Statements

For a Service Business	
Commissions and fees	$1,000,000
Selling, general, and administrative expenses	800,000
Operating income	200,000
Other income	25,000
Net income before provision for tax	225,000
Provision for income tax	65,000
Net income after income tax	$ 160,000

For a Manufacturing Business		
Gross income		$10,000,000
Materials	$5,700,000	
Direct labor	800,000	
Factory overhead	1,000,000	7,500,000
Gross margin (also called "gross profit")		2,500,000
Selling, general, and administrative expenses		2,000,000
Operating income		500,000
Other income		50,000
Net income before provision for income tax		550,000
Provision for income tax		165,000
Net income after income tax		$ 385,000

Exhibit 4-3
ABC Company
Comparative Statement of Income for the Years
Ended December 31, 20X4, and 20X5

		Dec. 31, 20X5		Dec. 31, 20X4
Sales (Net)		$3,075,000		$3,000,000
Cost of Sales		2,650,000		2,550,000
Gross Margin		$ 425,000		$ 450,000
Selling, General and Administrative				
Selling	$28,000		$25,000	
General and Administrative	40,000		43,000	
Other	20,000	88,000	25,000	93,000
Operating Income		$ 337,000		$ 357,000
Other Expenses				
Interest		45,000		55,000
Net Income Before Taxes		292,000		302,000
Tax (35%)		102,200		105,700
Net Income After Taxes		$ 189,800		$ 196,300
EPS (earnings per share)		$1.90		$1.96

Other revenue and expense items are listed below the operating income figure. These items are miscellaneous, nonrecurring, or unrelated to the primary operations of the organization. For example, if the organization earns revenue in the form of interest and dividends, or from rentals, royalties, and service fees, it would report them as other revenue. These items are then added (revenues) or subtracted (expenses) from operating income to determine the **net income before taxes**. After taxes have been deducted, the resulting figure is the **net income (or loss) after taxes**.

The final item on most income statements is **earnings per share (EPS)**. In a simple capital structure, EPS is calculated by dividing income after taxes by the total number of shares of common stock outstanding. For a complex capital structure, EPS is too complicated to be within the scope of this discussion.

The format of the ABC Company's income statement is known as the **multiple-step form**. This is by far the most widely used format. However, underwriters should be acquainted with the single-step format as well. In the single-step format, total expenses are deducted from total revenues to derive net income after taxes. There is no distinction between operating income and other income, or between selling, general, and administrative expenses and other expenses.

Financial Statement Analysis

Underwriters examine a company's financial records in the search for underwriting information about its financial health. The financial statements are of limited usefulness in and of themselves. However, several tools are available that transform these statements into useful information sources. These tools include (1) comparative financial statements; (2) percentage analysis, which includes trend percentages and vertical statement analysis; and (3) ratio analysis, discussed later in this chapter. These tools enable the underwriter to evaluate the financial data of a business by comparing it to a specific standard, called a benchmark. These standards include the company's past performance (trend analysis) and the performance of other companies in the same industry (industry analysis).

The most basic financial analysis tool is contained in **comparative financial statements**. Exhibits 4-1 and 4-3 presented the comparative financial statements of the ABC Company. If only the information as of December 31, 20X5, were presented, drawing valid conclusions about the company's financial strength would be difficult (unless the company were exceptionally strong or weak). For example, the ABC Company had a net income of $189,800 in 20X5. This fact by itself is not very useful. However, if the underwriter knew that the company had been earning an annual net income exceeding $500,000 for the previous five years, the current net income figure might indicate a possible moral or morale hazard or financial deterioration. If the company, on the other hand, had never earned more than $50,000 previously, the current income figure might indicate (1) a stronger and growing company, (2) a reduced likelihood of moral hazard, or (3) some nonrecurring transaction that affected income only in the single year.

Individual account classifications on all the statements can be compared in this manner as a means of obtaining useful underwriting information. For example, conclusions can be drawn by comparing inventory data found in the balance sheet from the past few years. The fact that the inventory of a company is currently valued at $1,000,000 is useful to the underwriter. Comparing the figure with several previous years' inventory levels would be much more meaningful and might reveal, for example, that inventories are increasing. An increasing inventory might be a sign of robust sales and healthy growth in the business. It could, on the other hand, indicate obsolete or damaged inventory, which might, in turn, indicate a moral hazard. That discovery might also indicate that a portion of the inventory will never be sold and converted into cash. The underwriter, however, must be sure that accounting principles have been consistently applied over the period of time covered by the comparison. A change in the method of inventory valuation, for example, can create false impressions, either of change or of stability.

Comparative financial statement analysis can be made easier by the use of **trend percentages**. This technique converts the dollar amounts to percentage increase or decrease relative to the base year. All dollar amounts in the base year are assigned a weight of 100 percent. The amounts in subsequent years are then expressed as percentages of the figures for the base year. Substituting percentages for large dollar amounts makes the results easier to read. Trend percentages are extremely useful in singling out unfavorable developments that might appear over time.

Common-size statements (or **vertical analysis**) are another financial analysis tool. They are useful when comparing the statements of two or more businesses, especially those of different size. Common-size balance sheets relate all values as percentages of total assets, and common-size income statements relate all values as a percentage of sales. A common-size balance sheet for the ABC Company is shown in Exhibit 4-4.

The underwriter should be careful not to confuse a vertical analysis percentage with trend analysis percentage. For example, inventories did not decrease by 2.91 percent from 20X4 to 20X5 (14.89 percent less 11.98 percent). The *percentage* of inventories to total assets, however, *did* decrease by that amount.

Such information can be particularly useful when compared to industry averages. Assume that the industry average for inventories is only 15 percent of total assets. This information might alert the underwriter to obsolete inventory and to a potential moral hazard. If the industry average for net property, plant, and equipment for companies with the same level of sales is only 55 percent (compared to the 74 percent level for the ABC Company), the ABC Company might be operating very inefficiently.

Financial tools such as comparative statements, trend percentages, and common-size statements are useful for interpreting accounting records. They allow underwriters to compare the current operations of a company against some standard of performance. By using the company's past performance and industry averages as standards, underwriters can obtain underwriting information and draw conclusions from these statements. An example of financial benchmarks is shown in Exhibit 4-5.

Exhibit 4-4
ABC Company Common-Size Balance Sheet

Assets	Dec. 31, 20X5	Dec. 31, 20X4
Current Assets		
Cash	1.60%	2.13%
Marketable Securities	3.59%	6.04%
Prepaid Expenses	0.40%	0.34%
Receivables (net)	8.58%	8.51%
Inventories	11.98%	14.89%
Total Current Assets	26.15%	31.91%
Net Property, Plant, and Equipment	73.85%	68.09%
Total Assets	100.00%	100.00%
Liabilities and Stockholders' Equity		
Current Liabilities		
Accounts Payable	3.19%	2.77%
Notes Payable	4.79%	4.26%
Accruals	.48%	.43%
Provisions for Federal Income Taxes	5.39%	5.53%
Total Current Liabilities	13.85%	12.99%
Mortgage Payable	24.95%	27.66%
Total Liabilities	38.80%	40.65%
Stockholders' Equity		
Capital Stock	39.92%	42.55%
Retained Earnings	21.28%	16.80%
Total Stockholders' Equity	100.00%	100.00%

Accounting Information From Alternative Sources

Underwriters should be aware that sources of accounting data other than financial statements exist. Although these sources are possibly less important than the financial statements themselves, they can supplement the statements and aid underwriters in gaining a more thorough understanding of a particular risk.

Exhibit 4-5
Benchmarks for Selected Industry Segments

Item Description for Accounting Period 7/96 Through 6/97	Other Special Trade Contractors	Business Services Except Advertising	Building Materials Dealers	Apparel and Accessory Stores
Number of Enterprises	15,912	27,737	2,450	6,966
Operating Costs/Operating Income (%)				
Cost of Operations	61.9	31.5	65.3	58.4
Taxes Paid	3.0	3.9	2.5	2.3
Interest Paid	0.8	0.6	0.5	0.7
Depreciation, Depletion, Amortization	2.3	1.7	1.3	1.0
Pensions and Other Benefits	1.8	1.5	0.9	0.2
Other	14.4	21.5	12.3	20.6
Officers' Compensation	6.1	10.0	4.9	4.3
Operating Margin	1.4	5.0	5.1	4.8
Oper. Margin Before Officers' Compensation	7.4	14.9	10.0	9.1
Selected Financial Ratios (Times to 1)				
Current Ratio	1.5	1.9	1.9	2.8
Quick Ratio	1.2	1.6	1.1	0.5
Net Sales to Working Capital	19.8	16.2	12.5	5.7
Total Asset Turnover	3.9	4.4	4.8	3.0
Inventory Turnover	•	•	8.7	2.6
Total Liabilities to Net Worth	1.8	1.4	1.5	1.5
Selected Financial Factors (%)				
Return on Assets	14.4	34.8	29.4	16.8
Return on Equity	29.7	•	•	32.0
Profit Margin, Before Income Tax	2.9	7.3	5.7	4.9
Profit Margin, After Income Tax	2.7	7.0	5.4	4.4

Adapted, with permission, from Leo Troy, *Almanac of Business and Industrial Financial Ratios*, 2000 Edition (Englewood Cliffs, NJ: Prentice Hall, 2000), pp. 30, 236, 254, and 320.

The Annual Report

One such source of information can be the annual report of a publicly held company. Various types of information are included in an annual report that enhance the financial statements themselves. The **annual report** briefly describes the company's background and growth. Usually, it also contains a summary and an analysis of the previous year's operation. Commonly, an annual report describes management's plans for the company and it contains charts, graphs, and ratios that aid the reader in understanding the financial data.

The management of the company prepares annual reports. As a result, the information is often biased in favor of the company. For example, managerial statements might present a more optimistic prediction of the future than is reasonable. Nevertheless, an underwriter can gain some insight into the financial condition of a company by reviewing its annual report.

The Prospectus

Another source of financial information concerning a company is its prospectus. A **prospectus** is a registration statement issued by the company for the purpose of describing a new security (stock or bond) issue. It must be filed with the Securities and Exchange Commission (SEC) at least twenty days before the new securities are publicly offered. A prospectus provides high-quality financial, legal, and technical information about the company. The major disadvantage of the prospectus is that it is prepared only if the company offers a new security issue.

The 10-K

The SEC requires all publicly traded companies to file an annual report updating their registration statement. This report is **Form 10-K**, which contains financial statistics and supplementary statements. The 10-K also contains a narrative section called **management's discussion and analysis (MD&A)**. This is a description of the firm's activities for the year, including comments about its financial condition and results of operations. A significant supplementary statement from an underwriting standpoint is the 10-K's listing of legal proceedings against the company. The SEC permits public access to this information through the Internet. Additionally, many libraries have SEC filing information on microfiche.

Other Sources of Information

In addition to the annual report, all companies registered with the SEC must also issue quarterly reports. These reports are not as detailed and are often not certified by a public (outside) accounting firm, but they can provide up-to-date information and help to determine the seasonal fluctuations of the business, especially inventory values. Underwriters can also obtain financial information about a company from sources that gather and report such information.

> **EDGAR—Electronic Data Gathering, Analysis, and Retrieval System**
> The SEC developed EDGAR to automate the collection, validation, indexing, acceptance, and forwarding of the financial information submitted to it by corporations. EDGAR provides a means of disseminating time-sensitive corporate information to investors and others that increases the efficiency and fairness of the securities market. Underwriters can access most of the information collected by EDGAR through the Internet.[1]

Shortcomings of Accounting Data

Before underwriters can use financial statements, they must understand the accounting data from which the statements are derived. Financial statements are most valuable when they are compared with the company's past financial statements, financial statements of similar companies, or applicable industry standards.

Variations in accounting methods make comparisons between financial statements difficult. Two companies of similar size might handle the same product lines, yet have entirely different items and amounts on their financial statements. These differences do not necessarily indicate that one company is financially stronger than the other. Different inventory methods result in different values for ending inventory, costs of sales, and gross profit, even though the same events took place during the same year.

For example, assume that Company X and Company Y both started business on January 1, 20X6. On that date, both purchased 10,000 widgets at $1.00 each. On July 1, 20X6, they each purchased 10,000 additional widgets at $1.20 each. Assume further that each company sold 15,000 widgets during the year at $1.25 each. Company X uses the first-in first-out (FIFO) method of valuing inventory, and Company Y uses the last-in first-out (LIFO) method.

The value of the ending inventory is derived by multiplying the number of units purchased by their purchase price and adding the result to the beginning inventory balance. The number of units taken out of inventory (sold) is multiplied by the assumed cost of the particular units taken out. The **FIFO method** assumes that the first items purchased are the first items sold. The **LIFO method** assumes that the last items brought into inventory are the first items taken out. In a period of rising prices, the LIFO method produces a higher cost of sales figure and therefore a smaller net income amount. For this reason, LIFO is used more frequently as a means of minimizing income taxes. The computation of the ending inventory, the cost-of-sales, and the gross profit for both companies are illustrated in Exhibit 4-6.

The accounting methods, procedures, and estimates that a particular company uses can be found either on the face of its statements or in a section of the statements normally entitled **Notes to the Financial Statements**. These notes are an integral part of the financial statements, and underwriters should not try to analyze the statements without reviewing the notes. The notes normally explain the accounting methods and estimates that the company uses for (1) notes payable, (2) income taxes, (3) long-term debt, (4) common stock, (5) stock options, (6) pension plans, (7) inventories, (8) retained earnings, (9) research and development costs, and (10) contingencies. Underwriters must remember that the notes are an important part of the financial statements and that the information contained in them is vital for interpreting accounting data presented in the statements.

Qualified Versus Unqualified Statements

Audited financial statements are generally considered more credible than unaudited ones. Audited statements are accompanied by an **audit report** prepared by an independent certified public accountant (CPA) that expresses a professional opinion as to the fairness of the company's statements. Underwriters should always review the auditor's report. An auditor may render three types of opinions: (1) unqualified, (2) qualified, and (3) adverse. The auditor may also disclaim an opinion. Auditors express opinions only on the financial statements, not on the entire annual report.

An **unqualified opinion** indicates that the financial statements have been examined and that they fairly present the financial position, the results of operations, and the changes in the financial position of a company. Such an opinion suggests that the statements are honest and free from bias and that the information contained in the statements is complete. An unqualified opinion also denotes that the company is using generally accepted accounting principles (GAAP) and applying them on a consistent basis. An unqualified opinion does not mean that the statements are "exactly correct," and it does not imply that there is no possibility of fraud. Fraud is, however, occasionally uncovered in the course of an audit.

If, in the auditor's opinion, the financial statements fairly present the financial condition of a company with only minor exceptions, a **qualified opinion** will

Exhibit 4-6
Computation of the Ending Inventory, the Cost of Goods Sold, and the Gross Profit

Company X—FIFO

Ending Inventory

	Quantity	Unit Cost	Total Cost
Purchase 1/1/20X6	10,000	$1.00	$10,000
Purchase 7/1/20X6	10,000	1.20	12,000
Sale 3/1/20X6	(10,000)	1.00	(10,000)
Sale 9/1/20X6	(5,000)	1.20	(6,000)
Balance	5,000		$ 6,000

Cost of Sales

Beginning Balance + Purchases – Ending Balance
  (0 + $22,000 – $6,000 = $16,000)

Gross Profit

Sales (15,000 × $1.25)	$18,750
Less Cost of Sales	16,000
Gross Profit	$ 2,750

Company Y—LIFO

Ending Inventory

	Quantity	Unit Cost	Total Cost
Purchase 1/1/20X6	10,000	$1.00	$10,000
Purchase 7/1/20X6	10,000	1.20	12,000
Sale 3/1/20X6	(10,000)	1.20	(12,000)
Sale 9/1/20X6	(5,000)	1.00	(5,000)
Balance	5,000		$ 5,000

Cost of Sales

Beginning Balance + Purchases – Ending Balance
  (0 + $22,000 – $5,000 = $17,000)

Gross Profit

Sales (15,000 × $1.25)	$18,750
Less Cost of Sales	17,000
Gross Profit	$ 1,750

be issued. Auditors commonly issue qualified opinions when a company has changed its inventory valuation method from the preceding year.

The auditor will issue an **adverse opinion** if the financial statements do not fairly present the financial position of a company. The auditor will also explain the reasons for this conclusion.

If an auditor cannot formulate an opinion for any reason, such as auditing restrictions imposed by the client or lack of independence, a **disclaimer** will be issued with the financial statements.

Ratio Analysis

Ratio analysis is an important tool in the study of the financial condition of an account. Ratio analysis uses data items found in the accounting records of a company and relates two or more of these items to one another so that the result can be compared to results for prior accounting periods or for similar businesses.

The first step in the use of ratios is to decide what information is needed for a particular account and then to choose the ratios that will provide this information in the most efficient manner. Hundreds of ratios can be produced from the data in the accounting records, but only a few are generally needed for a specific analysis. To identify which ratios to use, underwriters should not forget the objective of their financial analysis—the search for any information that will aid an underwriting decision. As discussed previously, underwriters use financial analysis to indicate (1) potential moral and morale hazards, (2) the account's ability to pay premiums, (3) financial strength and sound management, and (4) potential growth and possible future desirability from an underwriting standpoint.

Twelve ratios will be discussed in this chapter, but underwriters may need to examine only three or four when analyzing a particular company. The underwriter's area of concern will determine the particular ratios to use.

A ratio is a meaningless number in and of itself. To be useful, it must be compared in a logical manner with some baselines or guidelines. Normally, ratios are compared with (1) the same ratios of the company for past years to determine whether the company's performance is improving or deteriorating, (2) the ratios of other companies in the same industry to determine how the company compares with similar companies, or (3) the applicable industry benchmark. Key business ratios are available from some financial reporting organizations, such as Dun & Bradstreet.

Ratios must be used with caution. They are constructed from accounting data, and these data are subject to different interpretations and even to manipulation. Important factors to consider include inventory valuation methods, depreciation methods, and accounting for leases. Depending on which method is used, net income can be substantially modified.

Ratios generally can be classified into four basic groups:

- **Liquidity ratios**, which measure the company's ability to pay short-term obligations
- **Leverage ratios**, which measure the extent to which the company is financed with debt
- **Activity ratios**, which measure how well the company is using its assets
- **Profitability ratios**, which measure the degree to which the company is meeting its profitability goals

In the ratio examples that follow, the data are taken from the financial statements of the ABC Company that were presented in Exhibits 4-1 and 4-3.

Liquidity Ratios

Liquidity ratios measure the company's ability to pay its current maturing obligations. The ABC Company has obligations totaling $347,000 that must be paid within the next year (see Exhibit 4-1). Can this debt be paid? Is a strain on cash probable? Liquidity ratios can help answer these types of questions. A company with a low liquidity ratio is not in a good position to satisfy obligations (including insurance premiums) as they become due. Low and high are relative terms, of course. A ratio is useless unless it is compared to other ratios—either in trend analysis or in industry analysis. A high ratio indicates that the company is in a better position than its peers to pay its current premiums. Liquidity ratios can also help indicate a potential moral or morale hazard. An account with lower liquidity ratios might represent a moral hazard because of the temptation to intentionally cause a loss to receive cash. The most commonly used measures of liquidity are the current ratio, the quick ratio (also known as the **acid test ratio**), and working capital.

Current Ratio

The data used to determine the current ratio are found in the balance sheet. The ratio itself is computed by dividing current assets by current liabilities. Current assets typically include cash, marketable securities, accounts receivable, notes receivable, and inventories. Current liabilities normally include accounts and notes payable, the currently due portion of long-term debt, and accruals.

The current ratio indicates the extent to which assets that are expected to be converted to cash in the next year will cover the claims of short-term creditors. For example, a current ratio of 2:1 indicates that for every dollar of current debt, the company has two dollars of current assets. A current ratio of 2:1 has traditionally been considered satisfactory, but this is not an absolute rule.

The current ratio is calculated as follows:

$$\text{Current ratio} = \frac{\text{Current assets}}{\text{Current liabilities}}$$

Using the data in Exhibit 4-1 for the ABC Company yields the following:

$$\text{Current ratio for 20X4} = \frac{\$750,000}{\$305,000} = 2.5$$

and

$$\text{Current ratio for 20X5} = \frac{\$655,000}{\$347,000} = 1.9$$

The current ratio decreased because the ABC Company had fewer current assets with which to cover more current liabilities in 20X5 than in 20X4. If the average current ratio for the industry is 2.0, the ABC Company appears to be in line with that standard. Industry averages are often used for comparison; however, they are not necessarily the appropriate benchmark that all companies should try to achieve. The extent to which the business being analyzed represents the industry from which the average is calculated is crucial. In some industries, a few large companies greatly influence the average, in which case the average is less meaningful for the smaller companies in the industry. In the case of the ABC Company, even though the current ratio has decreased by 0.6, it is still very close to the industry average. Furthermore, with $1.90 worth of current assets for every $1.00 of current liabilities, the ABC Company should not have a liquidity problem, barring a dramatic adverse development in the near future. Consideration should be given, however, to how representative the ABC Company is of the average firm in the industry. If ABC's size or other characteristics greatly differ from the average, a different benchmark should be used for comparison, perhaps one developed from data of similarly sized firms within the industry.

Quick (Acid Test) Ratio

The quick ratio is similar to the current ratio. It is calculated by dividing the quick assets by the current liabilities. **Quick assets** include cash, readily marketable securities, and receivables. The only difference between quick assets and current assets is that the quick assets do not include inventory. The term "quick" is used to describe those assets that either exist in the form of cash or can quickly be converted into cash in order to pay current obligations. The quick ratio is calculated as follows:

$$\text{Quick ratio} = \frac{\text{Current assets less inventory}}{\text{Current liabilities}}$$

Using the data in Exhibit 4-1 for ABC Company yields the following:

$$\text{Quick ratio for 20X4} = \frac{\$400,000}{\$305,000} = 1.31$$

and

$$\text{Quick ratio for 20X5} = \frac{\$355,000}{\$347,000} = 1.02$$

In this illustration, every $1.00 worth of current debt was backed by $1.31 of cash or near-cash assets in 20X4 and by $1.02 of cash or near-cash assets in 20X5. Assume that the industry average is 1:1 (1:1 is the traditionally favorable level). Even though the quick ratio decreased in 20X5, it is still above the industry average. The company should be able to satisfy all current liabilities by liquidating its quick assets.

The quick ratio shows the extent to which the company could meet its obligations if it were to shut down or be liquidated immediately. A quick ratio of less than 1:1 is usually interpreted as a danger signal. Short-term creditors such as banks regularly use both quick and current ratios, and underwriters can use them as clear indicators of the financial well-being of a company.

Working Capital

Working capital is a measure of the extent to which current assets exceed current liabilities. Working capital is used to finance immediate operations, such as buy inventory, finance growth, and obtain credit.

Working capital is calculated as follows:

$$\text{Working capital} = \text{Current assets} - \text{Current liabilities}$$

Using the data in Exhibit 4-1 for the ABC Company yields the following:

$$\text{Working capital for 20X4} = \$750,000 - \$305,000$$
$$= \$445,000$$

and

$$\text{Working capital for 20X5} = \$655,000 - \$347,000$$
$$= \$308,000$$

ABC Company's working capital decreased by $137,000. Insufficient working capital can be detrimental to the operations and lead to the failure of a company. Surety bond underwriters perform a qualitative assessment of working capital on contractor accounts. Contractors often have financial resources but lack needed working capital to meet their current obligations. Surety bond underwriters review the individual categories of current assets and current liabilities to determine how much of the calculated amount of working capital would actually be accessible.

Leverage Ratios

Leverage ratios indicate the relationship between the amount of funds supplied by creditors and the funds supplied by the owners of the company. Leverage ratios can give the underwriter a feel for how the company is using borrowed funds, and they can indicate the financial strength of the company and the soundness of its management.

Leverage ratios reflect soundness—the greater the amount of debt, the greater the chance that the company will be unable to meet the required payments on the debt. Industry average ratios are particularly important for analysis of leverage, since the norm for use of debt financing varies greatly by industry. For example, industries with large amounts of property, plant, and equipment and fairly stable earnings can generally carry large amounts of debt. The public utility industry is a good example of a highly leveraged industry.

The three most commonly used leverage ratios are as follows:

- Total debt-to-total assets ratio
- Times interest earned ratio
- Fixed charge coverage ratio

Total Debt-to-Total Assets Ratio

The data used to calculate the **total debt-to-total assets ratio** are found in the balance sheet. The ratio is calculated by dividing total debt by total assets. The higher the ratio, the more funds creditors have supplied to the company's total financing. An exceptionally high ratio might indicate that the company has been financed too much by debt, and it might indicate financial weakness and doubtful growth. Under these circumstances, the underwriter must be aware of possible moral and morale hazards.

The total debt-to-total assets ratio is calculated as follows:

$$\text{Total debt-to-total assets ratio} = \frac{\text{Total debt}}{\text{Total assets}}$$

Using the data in Exhibit 4-1 for the ABC Company yields the following:

$$\text{Total debt-to-total assets ratio for 20X4} = \frac{\$955{,}000}{\$2{,}350{,}000} = 0.41$$

and

$$\text{Total debt-to-total assets ratio for 20X5} = \frac{\$972{,}000}{\$2{,}515{,}000} = 0.39$$

For every dollar of the company's assets in 20X5, creditors financed $.39. If the industry average for this ratio is $.35, the ABC Company is slightly above the average, but probably not high enough to cause concern.

Times Interest Earned Ratio

The number of times interest on borrowed funds is earned in a year is calculated by dividing earnings before interest payments and taxes (EBIT) by the interest charges. These data items are found in the income statement (see Exhibit 4-3). The **times interest earned ratio** is a good indicator of the debt-paying ability of a company because it measures the extent to which earnings can decline before the company is unable to pay annual interest costs. This is a key consideration when evaluating a company's financial strength.

The times interest earned ratio is calculated as follows:

$$\text{Times interest earned ratio} = \frac{\text{EBIT}}{\text{Interest charges}}$$

Using the data in Exhibit 4-2 for the ABC Company yields the following:

$$\text{Times interest earned ratio for 20X4} = \frac{\$357{,}000}{\$55{,}000} = 6.5 \text{ times}$$

and

$$\text{Times interest earned ratio for 20X5} = \frac{\$337{,}000}{\$45{,}000} = 7.5 \text{ times}$$

In 20X5, the ABC Company incurred interest charges of $45,000 and had an operating income of $337,000. In other words, the ABC Company earned enough to pay its interest charges 7.5 times. This is an improvement over 20X4. If the industry average were 8.0 times, the ABC Company would be below the average in 20X5, but improved over its previous year. An important factor to consider is the variability of earnings. If the company is in an industry in which earnings fluctuate widely from year to year, then this interest earned multiple should be large, allowing sufficient coverage of debt under a worst-case scenario. Stable earnings would permit a smaller multiple.

Fixed Charge Coverage Ratio

The sole difference between the times interest earned ratio and the fixed charge coverage ratio is that the latter includes lease and other fixed obligations. Lease obligations have similar characteristics to interest on debt obligations in that both must be paid. Therefore, the fixed charge coverage ratio is more inclusive and perhaps more important than the times interest earned ratio. The reason for the importance of this ratio is that a company can lease a facility rather than borrow money to purchase the same facility. Thus, rather than incurring an interest obligation, the company accepts the obligation to meet lease payments. Missing a lease payment can place the organization in financial difficulty just as severe as if an interest payment were missed. Any analysis of a company should thus include a measure for all fixed charges, rather than just interest charges. The data for this calculation are also found in the income statement. The ABC Company had no lease obligations. Therefore, this ratio is the same as the times interest earned ratio.[2]

The fixed charge coverage ratio is calculated as follows:

$$\text{Fixed charge coverage ratio} = \frac{\text{EBIT} + \text{Other fixed charges}}{\text{Interest charges} + \text{Other fixed charges}}$$

Using the data in Exhibit 4-3 for the ABC Company yields the following:

$$\text{Fixed charge coverage ratio for 20X4} = \frac{\$302{,}000 + \$0}{\$55{,}000 + \$0} = 5.5 \text{ times}$$

and

$$\text{Fixed charge coverage ratio for 20X5} = \frac{\$292{,}000 + \$0}{\$45{,}000 + \$0} = 6.5 \text{ times}$$

Activity Ratios

Activity ratios compare the level of sales with the account balance for various assets. Therefore, data from both the balance sheet and income statement (Exhibits 4-1 and 4-3) are needed to compute these ratios, which measure how effectively management employs its resources to produce sales.

The four common activity ratios are (1) the inventory turnover ratio, (2) the receivables turnover ratio, (3) the fixed assets turnover ratio, and (4) the total assets turnover ratio.

Inventory Turnover Ratio

The **inventory turnover ratio** indicates the number of times the inventory was replaced during the year. This ratio is calculated by dividing the cost of sales by the average inventory. The cost of sales is found in the income statement. The average inventory is the sum of the beginning and ending inventory (found in the comparative balance sheets) for the year, divided by two. The ABC Company, for the year 20X5, had a beginning inventory balance of $350,000 and an ending balance of $300,000. The average inventory for 20X5 was $325,000 [($350,000 + $300,000) / 2].

The inventory turnover ratio is calculated as follows:

$$\text{Inventory turnover ratio} = \frac{\text{Cost of sales}}{\text{Average inventory}}$$

Using the data above and in Exhibit 4-3 for the ABC Company yields the following:

$$\text{Inventory turnover ratio for 20X5} = \frac{\$2,650,000}{(\$350,000 + \$300,000)/2} = 8.2 \text{ times}$$

If the industry average is ten times, this company's inventory did not move as fast as inventory for the average firm. This could indicate obsolete merchandise, over-buying, or increases in prices over the year. The underwriter should be certain that the company did not change inventory policies during the year, which might result in incomparable beginning and ending inventory balances. The ABC Company's inventory turnover is probably not enough below the average to cause concern. However, if the turnover is well below the average, the underwriter should consider whether the account has obsolete inventory materials (items carried on the books at a cost much higher than their actual value). The company might be tempted to destroy the over-valued inventory intentionally to collect on an insured loss.

Receivables Turnover Ratio

The **receivables turnover ratio**, sometimes referred to as the **collection ratio**, measures the relationship between credit sales made during the year and the average amount of accounts receivable over the same period. Underwriters might have some difficulty obtaining the correct numerator for the ratio by simply examining the income statement. Specifically, the ratio's numerator calls for credit sales, but the income statement generally does not break down sales between credit and cash sales. Underwriters can check notes to the financial statement or other financial records to determine the amount of credit sales.

Assume that in 20X5 the ABC Company had $2,000,000 in credit sales and $1,075,000 in cash sales. The numerator for the ratio is $2,000,000. The calculation of the average accounts receivable is similar to the calculation of the average inventory previously described. The sum of the beginning and ending accounts receivable balance for the year is divided by 2.

The receivables turnover ratio is calculated as follows:

$$\text{Receivable turnover ratio} = \frac{\text{Credit sales}}{\text{Average accounts receivable}}$$

Using the data above and in Exhibit 4-1 for the ABC Company yields the following:

$$\text{Receivable turnover ratio for 20X5} = \frac{\$2,000,000}{\$200,000 + \$215,000 / 2} = 9.6 \text{ times}$$

This ratio can then be used to determine the average number of days an accounts receivable remains outstanding. This is found by simply dividing 365 by the receivables turnover ratio as follows:

$$\text{Average collection period} = \frac{365}{9.6} = 38 \text{ days}$$

The underwriter, by using these ratios, is looking for indications of poor collection policies on the part of management. The longer an account remains unpaid, the lower the likelihood of collection. Moreover, if the company has an average collection period that significantly exceeds the industry average, an early warning of financial problems might exist. That is, a company that has excess funds tied up in receivables might have difficulties in financing its other operations. Slow collections might indicate unsound management and possible financial weakness.

Writing off bad debts instead of collecting them might cause an improvement in the company's average collection period ratio. To determine if this is the case, the analyst would need to review changes in the account entitled "allowance for uncollectible accounts."

Fixed Assets Turnover Ratio

The **fixed assets turnover ratio** measures the number of times that sales of the year cover net property, plant, and equipment.

This ratio is calculated as follows:

$$\text{Fixed assets turnover ratio} = \frac{\text{Sales}}{\text{Average net property, plant, and equipment}}$$

Using the data in Exhibits 4-1 and 4-3 for the ABC Company yields the following:

$$\text{Fixed assets turnover ratio for 20X5} = \frac{\$3{,}075{,}000}{(\$1{,}600{,}000 + \$1{,}850{,}000) / 2} = 1.8 \text{ times}$$

This ratio shows the utilization level of plant and equipment. A low fixed asset turnover ratio can indicate excess capacity. This condition may be acceptable if it is only a temporary condition caused by a seasonal business cycle slow-down in sales. However, persistent excess capacity leads to possible moral hazard since a major fire is one way to reduce capacity quickly.

Total Assets Turnover Ratio

Underwriters also use the total assets turnover ratio to get a better idea of the financial strength and soundness of management. This ratio measures the turnover of the company's total assets instead of only the fixed assets.

The **total assets turnover ratio** is calculated by using the following formula:

$$\text{Total assets turnover ratio} = \frac{\text{Sales}}{\text{Average total assets}}$$

Using data in Exhibits 4-1 and 4-3 for the ABC Company yields the following:

$$\text{Total assets turnover ratio for 20X5} = \frac{\$3{,}075{,}000}{(\$2{,}350{,}000 + \$2{,}505{,}000) / 2} = 1.3 \text{ times}$$

The total assets turnover ratio is often used in year-to-year comparisons.

Profitability Measures

The ratios discussed thus far can furnish useful information about the capital structure and financial strength of a business. Profitability measures, on the other hand, measure the performance of a company.

Each of the three common profitability measures can be used to compare net profit after taxes to some other item on the balance sheet or income statement. Since a major goal of virtually all companies is to maximize net profit after taxes, profitability measures are good indicators of how well the company is achieving its goal. Even not-for-profit organizations strive to operate above a break-even position, indicating an application of sound management principles.

The three common profitability measures are as follows:

- Profit margin on sales
- Return on total assets
- Return on net worth

Profit Margin on Sales

The **profit margin on sales**, sometimes known as the **net profit ratio**, measures the net profit realized per dollar of sales. It is computed by dividing net income after taxes by sales. Both of these figures are found in the income statement.

The profit margin on sales ratio is calculated as follows:

$$\text{Profit margin on sales} = \frac{\text{Net income after taxes}}{\text{Sales}}$$

Using data in Exhibit 4-3 for the ABC Company yields the following:

$$\text{Profit margin on sales for 20X4} = \frac{\$196,300}{\$3,000,000} = 0.065 \text{ or } 6.5\%$$

and

$$\text{Profit margin on sales for 20X5} = \frac{\$189,800}{\$3,075,000} = 0.062 \text{ or } 6.2\%$$

In 20X5, the ABC Company realized a 6.2 percent net profit after taxes. This is a slight decrease compared to 20X4. Of course, a two-year time period is not adequate to develop a trend analysis. Normally, a minimum of five years should be used for useful trend analysis.

Assume that the average profit margin for the industry is 5 percent. The ABC Company is slightly above this average, which is a good indication. If the industry average is 10 percent, the underwriter should try to determine why the company's margin is substantially below the average.

This ratio is sometimes expressed as a before-tax figure. Using a before-tax figure allows businesses to show changes in its net profit ratio without the affect of tax law changes.

Return on Total Assets

This measure is computed by dividing net income after taxes by total assets. It measures the return on the total investment in the organization. Net income is found in the income statement, and total assets are found on the balance sheet.

The **return on total assets** is computed as follows:

$$\text{Return on total assets ratio} = \frac{\text{Net income after taxes}}{\text{Average total assets}}$$

Assuming that total assets from the 20X3 balance sheet was $2,200,000 and using data in Exhibits 4-1 and 4-3 for the ABC Company yields the following:

$$\text{Return on total assets for 20X4} = \frac{\$196,300}{(\$2,200,000 + \$2,350,000)/2} = 0.086 \text{ or } 8.6\%$$

and

$$\text{Return on total assets for 20X5} = \frac{\$189,800}{(\$2,350,000 + \$2,505,000)/2} = 0.078 \text{ or } 7.8\%$$

The reason for the decline from 20X4 to 20X5 is that ABC Company purchased more assets, and net income after taxes decreased. This might indicate that management made a poor decision in purchasing the assets. Again, two years are not enough time to develop a trend analysis, and this measure, like all ratios, should be used in conjunction with other return measures.

Return on Net Worth

This ratio measures the rate of return on net worth, which is found in the balance sheet. Net profit after taxes is used as the numerator.

The **return on net worth** is calculated as follows:

$$\text{Return on net worth} = \frac{\text{Net income after taxes}}{\text{Average net worth}}$$

Assuming that total net worth from the 20X3 balance sheet was $1,205,000 and using data in Exhibits 4-1 and 4-3 for the ABC Company yields the following:

$$\text{Return on net worth ratio for 20X4} = \frac{\$196,300}{(\$1,205,000 + \$1,395,000)/2} = 0.151 \text{ or } 15\%$$

and

$$\text{Return on net worth ratio for 20X5} = \frac{\$189,800}{(\$1,395,000 + \$1,533,000)/2} = 0.1296 \text{ or } 13\%$$

In many respects, return on net worth ratio is the most important profitability measure because it measures actual return to the stockholders (owners), net of the effect of financial leverage—unlike the gross return measure, return on total assets. If this measure is lower than the industry average, the other ratios can be used to diagnose where the problem or problems are. Too much money might be tied up in capital because of poor inventory management or a poor credit collection policy. The company might be operating at a too-low percentage of capacity, which would be made evident by the total assets turnover ratio and the fixed assets turnover ratio. Finally, the company might have too much debt or be paying too high an interest rate for it. Leverage ratios, discussed earlier, would diagnose these problems.

Summary

Generally, well-managed businesses are better accounts for underwriters than those that are poorly managed. Underwriters often rely on an account's financial information to evaluate management competence and possibly detect a moral hazard.

The balance sheet and income statement are the financial statements most commonly used to analyze businesses. The balance sheet shows what a business owns and what it owes. The accounting equation expresses the relationship of the major categories on the balance sheet: assets = liabilities + owners' equity. While the balance sheet shows the financial position of a business at one point in time, the income statement provides a financial summary of operations for a period of time. The income statement begins with the firm's sales, which are reduced for expenses such as cost of good sales and selling, general, and administrative expenses to determine net income. The net gain or loss (net income) shown in the income statement ties to the owners' equity category of the balance sheet by increasing or decreasing retained earnings.

Financial statements need to be analyzed to provide useful information. One approach is trend analysis, in which the current financial results are compared with past results. Another approach is industry analysis, in which a company's financial results are compared with other companies in the same industry classification. Specific analysis tools include comparative statements and ratio analysis.

This chapter highlights the balance sheet and income statement, yet many businesses produce other financial reports that may be useful to the underwriter. Many of these financial reports are also publicly accessible. The annual report is the company's report to stockholders. The prospectus is a registration statement required by the SEC when a company offers new securities to the public. The 10-K is an annual report required by the SEC of all companies that are publicly traded.

Accounting rules permit companies some flexibility in reporting financial information to reflect the varied business operations that GAAP accounting rules encompass. Sometimes the latitude permitted is relatively small, such as whether the company uses LIFO or FIFO for measuring inventory. In other instances, accounting information can be misused in such a way as to make the company appear to be in better shape financially than it is. Independent certified public accountants perform audits to determine whether the company's financial statements fairly represent the company's financial condition. CPA opinions may be unqualified, qualified, or adverse.

Ratio analysis uses information from the balance sheet and income statement to compare current financial results with prior financial results or with the financial results of other companies in the same industry. Financial ratios are categorized into four basic groups: liquidity ratios, leverage ratios, activity ratios, and profitability measures.

Chapter Notes

1. Home page for EDGAR, World Wide Web: http://www.sec.gov/edgarhp.htm
2. In some cases, payments made toward the principal of a loan are also included, since many firms consider repayment of principal to be close to mandatory. If added, the payments have to be converted to a before-tax basis since they are not deductible.

Chapter 5

Pricing the Insurance Product

Pricing means setting a price for a product or service and establishing the terms and conditions for the insurance agreement. Underwriters have the primary role in individual account pricing. Actuaries, as mentioned in Chapter 1, use mathematical techniques to establish insurance rates for the insurer's book of business, which underwriters apply to individual accounts. Actuarial pricing activities, usually referred to as ratemaking, are described in *Advanced Underwriting Techniques*. Underwriting pricing activities usually include account classification, rating, and application of applicable premium modification plans.

The roles of individual underwriters in underwriting pricing activities vary from insurer to insurer and from one line of business to another. Some insurers have underwriting technicians who classify and rate accounts at the direction of the underwriter. Underwriters at other insurers perform the classification and rating function as part of their underwriting tasks. Marine and specialty underwriters usually have extreme flexibility in account pricing and can develop rates without actuarial intervention. Regardless of their individual role in pricing activities, underwriters try to ensure that the premium an account is charged is sufficient for the risk assumed.

Underwriters spend a significant amount of their time on risk assessment, but pricing is often as important. Applicants, through their agent or broker, usually request quotes from several insurers. Differences among insurers and their products are often difficult for the applicant to assess, so they make their decision to buy insurance based primarily on price. Underwriters need to be aware of competitive conditions in the market and recognize the effect of soft and hard markets on insurance pricing. Underwriters also need to realize that they can be too competitive on price. An inadequately priced book of business threatens insurers' solvency.

Pricing the insurance product is different from pricing most other products and services because the underlying costs of insurance products (chiefly, the losses that will occur during the policy period) are not known before the sale. This chapter describes the mathematical basis for insurance pricing, constraints on insurance pricing, the rating process, and methods used to tailor the price of insurance to a particular account.

The Law of Large Numbers

The law of large numbers is the mathematical principle that makes risk transference possible. Risk transference through insurance allows members of a group or pool to exchange the uncertainty of economic loss for the certainty of insurance premium payment. Insurance is able to reduce the uncertainty of the individual members of the pool by increasing the predictability of the pool as a whole.

The law of large numbers explains how pooling increases predictability and the conditions that must be met for it to operate properly. According to the law of large numbers, adapted for insurance purposes, when the number of similar independent exposure units increases, the relative accuracy of predictions about future losses based on these exposure units also increases.

An **exposure unit** is a fundamental measure of the loss exposure assumed by the insurer. For example, actuaries use car-year as the exposure unit for auto insurance—one auto insured for a twelve-month period. In simple terms, actuaries divide total losses and loss adjustment expenses by the number of exposure units to determine loss costs per unit of exposure. While car-year is the appropriate exposure unit or exposure base for auto insurance, other lines of insurance use exposure bases that are responsive to the characteristics of the insurance being provided. Rating manuals used by underwriters and underwriting technicians for individual account pricing often use the term exposure basis interchangeably with premium base. **Premium base** is the exposure unit denominated into a variable that approximates the loss potential for a line of insurance, such as gross sales, payroll, admissions, total cost, units, and amount of insurance in hundreds or thousands.

Underwriting account selection activities are critical to the proper operation of the law of large numbers. In addition to having a large number of exposure units, viable risk transference requires that exposure units be independent and homogenous. Underwriters, through exposure analysis and classification, help ensure that these conditions are met. The importance of these conditions is explained below.

Origin of the Law of Large Numbers

During the seventeenth century, many mathematicians, including Blaise Pascal, studied games of chance and developed the rules of combinations, permutations, and other aspects of probability. As the work of Descartes, Newton, and Leibnitz led to the development of calculus, mathematics became increasingly formal. That is, mathematicians tried not only to infer previously unrecognized relationships (rules), but also to develop logical proofs to demonstrate these relationships convincingly.

The great Swiss mathematician, Jacob Bernoulli, developed the first proof (published posthumously in 1713) of a rule that is the basis for the modern practice of insurance. Bernoulli considered this rule, which has come to be known as the law of large numbers, to be well-known already. "For even the most stupid of men," he wrote, "by some instinct of nature, by himself and without any instruction (which is a remarkable thing), is convinced that the more observations have been made, the less danger there is of wandering from one's goal."[1] Bernoulli's formal proof of the law of large numbers not only demonstrated that uncertainty can be reduced by increasing the number of observations but also showed how the principle could be quantified.[2]

Homogeneity

The operation of the law of large numbers is predicated on the exposure units being similar or **homogeneous**. Exposure units need not be identical, but they should face approximately the same expected frequency and severity of loss. Homogeneity is ensured through classification systems and the refinement of those systems.

Insurance classification systems group risks that share similar characteristics and that usually have the same likelihood of loss. Categories created by separate lines of business such as general liability and commercial property also help improve the homogeneity of the events that might cause a loss.

The operation of the law of large numbers can be improved by further refining the classification system used, even if it means reducing the number of exposure units in each classification. The definition of the law of large numbers states that prediction accuracy increases as the number (*n*) of exposure units increases. However, as *n* increases into the thousands, further increases in the number of risks provide smaller and smaller improvements in predictive accuracy.[3]

Loss Frequency and Loss Severity

Underwriters usually analyze the potential loss exposures of an account in terms of loss frequency and loss severity. Such an analysis should disclose the profit potential of the account and how improvements in the account's profit potential might be achieved.

Loss frequency refers to the number of losses that occur in a particular period. Employees of a garment manufacturer, for example, might suffer a series of minor lacerations caused by cutting and sewing equipment. Likewise, a bakery account with a large fleet of delivery trucks is likely to have multiple minor accidents. Other types of losses, such as those caused by earthquakes, hurricanes, and fire, occur much less frequently.

Underwriters are particularly interested in loss frequency because loss frequency can often be controlled. Frequent puncture-wound losses might be eliminated or reduced by the installation of machine guards or changes in materials-handling procedures. Frequent fender-benders caused by one driver might be controlled by firing that driver or assigning him or her to other work. Underwriters often try to shift the burden of small but frequent losses back to the insured by setting deductibles at such a level that the insured retains these losses.

Loss severity is the dollar amount of damage that results or might result from each loss exposure. Gauging the potential severity of property losses is easier than gauging the potential severity of liability losses. Most property losses have a finite value, and whether the property is partially or completely destroyed, the severity of the loss is usually calculable. The severity of liability exposures is much harder to calculate. If a paint manufacturer, for example, sells paint that produces toxic fumes when applied, the severity of the potential liability loss is almost unlimited.

Underwriters are usually required to make an estimate of an account's loss severity when evaluating an account. Unlike with loss frequency, analysis of past losses is less helpful when evaluating loss severity.

Actuaries and underwriters try to identify additional attributes that affect or reflect potential frequency and severity of loss. Actuaries are often able to use this information in the creation of a more refined classification system that produces more accurately priced accounts. Underwriters look for these attributes during the underwriting process so that they can select the superior accounts within a classification.

The goal of actuaries and underwriters when designing a rating system is to make each class as homogeneous as possible without sacrificing the predictive accuracy that large numbers create. The amount of confidence an actuary has in projected losses (and the resulting rates) increases as the number of exposure units increases. Actuaries call this confidence level **credibility**. Credibility factors vary from zero (no credibility at all) to one (full confidence). Credibility factors are used to minimize variations in rates that result from purely chance variations in losses. One simple way of applying credibility is to multiply the projected rate change by the credibility factor. For example, if the credibility factor is .30 and the data indicate that a rate increase of 10 percent is needed, a rate increase of 3 percent ($10 \times .30$) would be taken. This same approach would be used for rate reductions so that those rates become stabilized over time.

Independence

For the law of large numbers to operate properly, events should be independent of one another. **Independence** means that the occurrence of one event has no effect on the likelihood of the occurrence of any other event. Independence is not maintained when more than one exposure unit is exposed to the same loss-causing event. For example, one catastrophic event, such as an earthquake, a hurricane, or a flood, can affect many exposure units. Insurers often insure multiple buildings that are adjacent to one another. Because of their proximity, a fire in one building could spread to the other structures, thereby violating the condition of independence.

While the condition of independence is frequently violated, underwriters have an important role in evaluating the independence of exposure units insured. Insurers usually use information systems to track the geographic location of properties insured. In addition to designating the geographic location of each insured property, underwriters are usually required to determine an amount subject for each location. The **amount subject** measures the exposure to a single loss. Insurers differ in their approach to calculating each account's amount subject, but the objective is to determine potential loss severity. For example, an insurer might require its underwriters to assume a total loss and determine the maximum dollar amount that could possibly be paid for all responding coverages. Insurers aggregate this information using catastrophe-modeling computer software to determine total amounts subject to various types of catastrophes. Underwriters use this information to limit their exposures in certain geographic areas or obtain catastrophe reinsurance.

Most insurers use reinsurance to decrease their catastrophic exposure. Under such an arrangement, an insurer pays a reinsurer a premium to reimburse the insurer for losses above a specified retention. Catastrophe protection is only one of several functions that reinsurance can serve for insurers. Reinsurance is described in *Advanced Underwriting Techniques*.

Ideally Insurable Loss Exposures[4]

In addition to the conditions included in the law of large numbers, insurers consider other characteristics when determining whether a loss exposure is commercially insurable.

Losses That Are Accidental. An ideally insurable loss exposure involves a potential loss that is accidental from the standpoint of the insured. If the insured has some control over whether a loss will occur, the insurer is at a disadvantage because the insured might have an incentive to cause a loss. If losses are not accidental, the insurer cannot calculate an appropriate premium because the chance of a loss could increase as soon as a policy is issued. If the loss exposure involves only accidental losses, the insurer can better estimate future losses and calculate an adequate premium for the exposure.

Losses That Are Definite and Measurable. To be insurable, a loss should have a definite time and place of occurrence, and the amount of loss must be measurable in dollars. Insurable loss exposures should be definite and measurable for practical reasons. If the time and location of a loss cannot be definitely determined and the amount of the loss cannot be measured, writing an insurance policy that defines what claims to pay and how much to pay for them becomes extremely difficult. Also, losses are impossible to predict if they cannot be measured. For example, the sudden bursting of a water pipe that causes water damage is an occurrence that has a definite time and place and that can thus be insured. However, if a slow leak in the pipe causes decay and rotting over several years, the resulting loss does not have a definite time of occurrence and is generally not insurable.

Losses That Are Economically Feasible to Insure. Insurers seek to cover only loss exposures that are economically feasible to insure. Because of this constraint, loss exposures involving small losses as well as those involving a high probability of loss are generally considered uninsurable. Writing insurance to cover small losses does not make sense when the expense of providing the insurance probably exceeds the amount of potential loss. Insurance to cover the disappearance of office supplies, for example, could require the insurer to spend more to issue claim checks than it would to pay for claims. It also does not make sense to write insurance to cover losses that are almost certain to occur. In such a situation, the premium would probably be as high as or higher than the potential amount of the loss. For example, insurers generally do not cover damage due to wear and tear because such damage normally occurs over time.

Constraints on Insurance Pricing

Insurers must comply with the rate regulatory laws in each state in which they write insurance. Additionally, insurers are also often required to satisfy social concerns even though they are not included in state statutes. Rate regulation satisfies two goals of insurance regulation: solvency and equity.

Regulatory Objectives

Although the objectives of rate regulation are generally the same for all states, the approaches used differ significantly. Rate regulation serves three general objectives:

- To ensure that rates are adequate
- To ensure that rates are not excessive
- To ensure that rates are not unfairly discriminatory

Adequate

Rates must be adequate in order for the premiums collected to be sufficient to pay for incurred losses and the expenses associated with those losses. Rate regulatory laws include the adequacy criterion because of the tendency of insurers to engage in destructive competition. Because rates are based on predictions of future losses, insurers have often been willing to establish prices that win market share, but that lead to their insolvency. Of the three regulatory criteria, rate adequacy is the most important.

Insurance regulators recognize that achieving rate adequacy requires that insurers be allowed to engage in collective ratemaking. Concerted ratemaking allows insurers to pool ratemaking statistics to improve the predictability of losses and thereby the likelihood that rates are adequate.

Pooling ratemaking statistics to create standard insurance industry rates would be a clear violation of the Sherman Act and other federal antitrust laws if it were not for the enactment by Congress of the McCarran-Ferguson Act. The **McCarran-Ferguson Act** preserved state regulation of insurance after the United States Supreme Court ruled that insurance was subject to federal regulation.[5] While affirming the right of the federal government to regulate insurance, the McCarran-Ferguson Act enabled state regulation to continue as long as insurance was adequately regulated by the states. The McCarran-Ferguson Act exempted the insurance industry from the Sherman Act and other federal antitrust laws.[6]

With help from the insurance industry, the National Association of Insurance Commissioners (NAIC) approved a model rate regulation act in 1947. This model act called for prior approval of a wide class of rates with specific criteria—specifically that they be adequate, not excessive, and not unfairly discriminatory—that should be used to approve rates. After the enactment of the McCarran-Ferguson Act, every state passed some form of rate regulation statute. To preempt federal antitrust laws, an explicit state regulatory policy displacing competition was needed. Therefore, states specified the limits to which insurers could cooperate in data gathering and form filing.[7]

Insurers use insurance advisory organizations to facilitate cooperative ratemaking. As mentioned in Chapter 1, insurance advisory organizations voluntarily discontinued the practice of determining final rates in the 1980s.[8] State and federal policymakers criticized this practice. Additionally, a major lawsuit was initiated over this practice by nineteen state attorneys general charging that insurance advisory organization development of final rates was anticompetitive. Limiting their ratemaking function to developing prospective loss costs—rates that do not include a provision referred to as a loading for insurer expenses or profits—was one of the changes insurance advisory organizations made to address this criticism and settle the lawsuits.

Cooperatively developed loss costs, although they address the criticism about developing final rates, do not necessarily ensure rate adequacy. Prospective loss costs for a particular classification might be adequate *on average* for all accounts in that classification, but not necessarily for the specific accounts an insurer writes. Underwriters need to have a sense of the attributes of the average account contemplated in a classification to determine whether the class rate is adequate for it. Additionally, underwriting guidelines reflect underwriting management's desire to write many accounts, but a limited number of classifications. Having many accounts in a classification helps ensure that the class rate is adequate for the insurer.

The rate regulatory constraints—adequate, not excessive, and not unfairly discriminatory—were established so that insurance market competition would be the primary regulator of rates. Underwriters should be aware of the competitive pressures that exist in the soft market and the tendency to price accounts lower than they should be priced. Insurers often use underwriting information systems to determine whether pricing adjustments have underpriced a book of business. Underwriters use these systems to identify potentially underpriced accounts and make corrective pricing adjustments when market conditions change.

In balancing regulatory goals, regulators have sometimes sacrificed the regulatory objective of rate adequacy for the social objective of affordability. Insurance regulators, in these instances, have decided that insurers should subsidize one line of insurance with another rather than charge the rate considered to be adequate to insureds. Maintaining rates at artificially low rate levels has most frequently occurred in personal auto insurance and workers compensation insurance.

Not Excessive

A rate is considered **not excessive** if it does not generate an *unreasonable* profit for the insurer. What constitutes an unreasonable profit has been difficult to define.[9] Because of the uncertainty associated with insurance pricing, insurance regulators and insurers are usually unable to determine whether the proposed rates will yield an unreasonable profit. Insurance regulators usually rely on competition in the insurance marketplace to ensure that rates are not excessive.[10] In some states, if it is determined that the insurer made an excessive profit, the excess profit must be returned to consumers or remitted to the state. This rate regulatory criterion helps ensure that insurers do not take advantage of the insurance-buying public for a product considered to be essential.

Not Unfairly Discriminatory

A rate is **not unfairly discriminatory** if it equitably reflects the expected losses and expenses of the insured to whom it applies. An equitable share is generally based on some measure of the insured's perceived measure of future losses and expenses. The emphasis of this criterion is on *unfairly*. Differences in the prices charged for different accounts should be based on an actuarially sound basis. Accounts that present the same likelihood of loss should be charged approximately the same rate.

Classification plans help insure rate equity by grouping insureds with similar loss potential. Absolute rate equity would mean that each account would be charged a rate that reflects its own losses and expenses. A risk transference program based on absolute rate equity would not be insurance because there would be no risk sharing. Insurance involves pooling of risk; a

Regulation Administration[11]

Insurance regulators usually use one of the following approaches to administer rate regulatory laws.

Prior approval. Prior approval generally means that the rate and supporting rules must be approved by the regulator before they can be used in that state. In some cases, a "deemer provision" in the law says that a filing is deemed approved if the insurer has not heard from the regulator within a given time period (usually from thirty to ninety days).

File and use. Under file and use systems, the insurer must file rates and rules within a specified time before use (usually from thirty to ninety days). That time period gives the regulator a minimal opportunity to uncover violations of law or other practices that might be challenged.

Use and file. Under use and file laws, the insurer can use any rate it wants, provided that the insurer files the rate with the regulator within thirty to sixty days after the rate is put into use. The regulator then has a reasonable period in which to review the rate and to request a hearing to disapprove the rate.

Open competition. Open competition, also called no file, allows insurers to develop and use rates without having to get approval or to file with state regulators. Open competition is officially the regulatory practice in only a handful of states and then only for some lines of insurance.

State mandated. Some states set the rates insurers use. If insurers do not use the mandated rates, they can be penalized.

Hybrids of these filing approaches exist. For example, open competition might apply as long as certain tests are met, such as evidence of competitive markets or rate increases of less than 25 percent per year. Failing to satisfy these criteria means that prior approval or another regulatory review might apply.

Many states have enacted statutes exempting insurers from filing rates and forms for large commercial accounts. Insurers will, however, need to file rates and forms—using the applicable administrative procedures described above—for commercial accounts that do not meet the exemption requirements.

risk transference program based on absolute rate equity would be a form of forced budgeting. Retrospective rating, an individual rating plan described later in this chapter, is often referred to as a "cost-plus" insurance program. Accounts that are priced with a retrospective rating program do pay for their own losses, but the account's contribution is limited to the maximum premium cap selected by the insured.

Assuming that classification plans are devised to provide equitable treatment of insureds, underwriters can help ensure equity in pricing by properly classifying accounts. Unfair discrimination *might* occur in the development of a rate, but it is *more likely* to occur when accounts are misclassified, purposely or not, and when individual rate modification factors applied to manual rates are unjustified. Discriminating among accounts is central to the underwriter's task of account selection. Fair and justified discrimination permits underwriters to offer better pricing to better accounts.

Social Criteria

Society imposes rules of conduct on its members, and those rules extend to setting rates for insurance. Among the social concerns that influence insurance departments are the availability of insurance, the public's ability to pay the premium, simplicity in rating structures, and the insured's ability to control the factors used for classification and rating.

Availability

Some accounts have experienced trouble obtaining insurance coverage or obtaining insurance at an affordable price—effectively making the insurance unavailable. The social goal of **availability** means that insurance is accessible to those who want or need it.

As described in Chapter 1, insurers have a limited capacity and they usually allocate that capacity to maximize their return on equity. Because of this limitation, insurers want their underwriters to select those accounts that have the greatest likelihood of producing a profit.

Availability problems also occur when insurance rates are too low. Some accounts in a classification may be determined to be unprofitable and thereby undesirable from an underwriter's perspective. In some instances, specific classes as a whole may be proven to be underpriced and likewise are avoided. Additionally, in some lines of business, the rates may be artificially held at a level at which insurers cannot make a profit. Such might be the case when insurance regulators have rejected price increases.

The cyclical nature of insurance creates periodic shortages of insurance. The insurance industry moves from periods of profits—in which prices are reduced and coverage is generally more available—to periods of losses—in which prices are increased and the coverage availability is reduced. The cyclical nature of insurance is a consequence of competition in the insurance marketplace. In a competitive market, insurers operate efficiently to restrict insurance availability where it might be unprofitable.

Affordability

An important emerging criterion for insurance rates is affordability. **Affordability** can mean (1) that a ceiling is placed on insurance rates so that people who need coverage can purchase it, (2) that rates are determined so that they transfer a portion of the costs of coverage from high-risk insureds to the remaining insureds, or (3) that a subsidy from outside the insurance mechanism offsets the actuarially determined premiums that are deemed unaffordable.

Insurance affordability problems are evident in many urban areas where the cost of commercial property insurance has risen even as property values have declined. Many insurers have rejected accounts located in urban areas for newer, better protected properties located in suburban communities. Deteriorating loss experience, urban decay, a declining tax base, rising crime rates, and a host of other circumstances have been cited as at least partial causes of the rise in the cost of insurance and the reluctance of insurers to provide coverage. Insurance for many inner-city accounts is effectively unavailable because it is not affordable.

Availability problems often result from disasters as well. Many insurers withdrew from writing policies in coastal counties after Hurricane Andrew. In turn, lenders will not provide funds to businesses when insurance is unavailable. Insurance availability is in part relative to its affordability. Likewise, insurance regulators cannot ignore the social implications of affordability and availability.

Simplicity

An additional social criterion for ratemaking is **simplicity**. A rate must be reasonably simple to develop and modify. That criterion is a function of the insurance industry's data development and administrative capabilities as well as of the insurance industry's need to explain and defend its system to the public. Many states require that rate changes be accompanied by complete actuarial data before the change can be implemented.

Assume, for example, that an insurer's commercial auto rating system bases its rate on the number of miles driven per year by each vehicle in each rating territory in the state. The insurer must determine from each insured not only the number of miles driven but also exactly where the mileage was logged. Such a rating system might be feasible as more vehicles become equipped with geographic positioning technology that would make the capture of this information cost effective. In the meantime, the administrative expenses involved make this system cost prohibitive.

Controllability

Control over rating factors has recently emerged as a social criterion for insurance rates. Consumer advocates maintain that insureds should not have to pay a higher premium because of factors over which they cannot exercise control. While this debate has focused primarily on the use of age and gender in personal auto insurance pricing, similar pressure could be brought to bear in commercial lines.

Other Criteria

Other insurer objectives affect the pricing of insurance. Insurers want rates to encourage their insureds to control losses. They also want rates to be responsive to changes in conditions that affect losses and expenses, yet rates should remain relatively stable.

Encourage Loss Control

Many insurers have pricing methodologies that encourage and reward loss control practices. Giving accounts an incentive to practice loss control is important to insurers because the objective of loss control is to reduce the frequency and severity of losses. Because insurers cannot determine what losses *did not occur* because of loss control measures or which losses are *less severe than they otherwise would be*, the benefits of loss control are often intangible. Accounts are often convinced of the value of loss control measures when their insurers recognize their efforts through price reductions. Accounts, for example, that are not required by the applicable building code to install sprinkler systems are often persuaded to do so after they understand the extent of their potential property insurance premium reduction.

Responsive

Rates should respond in a timely manner to changes affecting the likelihood of losses. Most claims occur and are resolved quickly so that appropriate increases and decreases in rates can occur soon after the experience period. In some lines of business, a loss can take years to resolve so that an insurer's ultimate loss payment, if any, will be unknown until a settlement is reached or a court renders a decision. Because insurers cannot wait years to determine the adequacy of their rates, actuaries use trend factors to adjust rates to include changes in costs that underlie insurance claims, such as medical costs.

Underwriters use pricing to attract superior accounts and deter undesirable accounts. If rates are not responsive, underwriters will likely develop under-priced books of business or be unable to meet their production goals.

Stability

Insureds want stability in insurance pricing; rates should not fluctuate significantly from year to year. **Stability** implies that rates should remain firm and change only when underlying costs have changed substantially, thereby justifying a change. As mentioned, credibility factors are used to minimize the effect of loss experience so that indicated rate changes are less abrupt.

The public has endured instability in the insurance marketplace during periods in which insurance coverage was unaffordable. Physicians had diffi-culty obtaining affordable professional liability insurance during the late 1970s. Commercial liability rates in general increased dramatically during the 1980s. Similar problems with insurance affordability have occurred in personal lines. Pricing instability usually means that the competitive mar-ketplace is not operating effectively, inviting regulatory intervention.

The Rating Process

The rating and proper pricing of accounts are among the main responsibilities of commercial lines underwriters. Understanding rating procedures is vital to making good underwriting decisions. **Rating** means applying rates and rating plans to the exposure units of insureds. The rating process consists of the following steps:

- Determining the specific plans under which individual applicants or groups of applicants are eligible
- Selecting the appropriate classifications for those particular applicants
- Applying rates to the proper number of exposure units
- Applying individual rating plans to arrive at the final premium

In addition, underwriters must evaluate the nonquantifiable factors that are not part of the rating process but that might affect the loss potential of an account.

Rate Manuals

A **rate manual** contains the rates or loss costs for every classification as well as all the necessary rules, factors, and guidelines to apply those rates. Rate manuals provide a source of information for classifying accounts and developing premiums for given types of insurance. Once the classification groupings and the premiums are determined, that information can assist the underwriter in the selection decision by answering the question, "Are we getting enough premium for the potential losses we are insuring?"

In addition, the rate manual provides important information concerning the use of endorsements that amend the policy. Endorsements that broaden coverage or reduce coverage can be competitive tools that help underwriters obtain and retain accounts with a better-than-average loss potential. Restrictive endorsements are often necessary to solve underwriting problems and to make accounts acceptable. Rate manuals contain the rules for using endorsements to tailor coverage to individual accounts.

Rate manuals have some limitations. First, they do not always contain an appropriate class or rate for each account. Second, loss exposures change over time, and the rules, procedures, and rates taken from manuals might not always satisfy the underwriter's requirements, even though the manuals are frequently updated or are provided through an online computer service. Finally, the manual might not cover certain loss exposures for a given account. That is, the manuals used by most underwriters contain relatively little discussion of the loss exposures underlying the classifications themselves. Thus, underwriters must augment information found in rate manuals.

Classification

Generally, the rate that is applied to an individual account is determined primarily by the account's classification. When an account with unique characteristics is submitted to the insurer, the underwriter might use discretion in determining the category or classification into which the account is placed. That discretion might create a temptation to use classification as a competitive tool. Sometimes, the correct classification requires some judgment in determining the insured's primary business. However, commercial classification systems are comprehensive, and almost all accounts fit logically into a given class. These classification systems are designed to expedite pricing and tend to reflect a logical approach. Extensive footnotes, for instance, help guide underwriters to the appropriate classification when more than one classification might seem to apply. Placing two accounts that are in the same business into different classes is a form of unfair discrimination and against the law. State insurance examiners look for that type of unfair discrimination during market conduct examinations, and examiners will impose fines if they find a pattern of unfair discrimination.

Consequently, underwriters must know the ratemaking and classification systems and thoroughly understand the interdependence of the two systems.

In addition, underwriters must remember that the proper classification of accounts is directly related to the accuracy of underwriting information. If the information is not verified, an account can be misclassified, resulting in excessive or inadequate premium. For example, incorrect information on the type of product the insured manufactures might result in a rate that is too low for the exposure.

Market Conduct Examinations[12]

Market conduct regulation focuses on insurers' treatment of insureds, applicants for insurance, and claimants, with oversight in four areas of insurer operations: sales and advertising, underwriting, ratemaking, and claim settlement. Market conduct regulation is performed through **market conduct examinations**. Market conduct examiners might look for one or more of the following activities during a market conduct examination of underwriting.[13]

- Unfair discrimination in underwriting practices
- Improper cancellation and nonrenewal
- Failure to file rates or forms or both
- Inaccurate application of filed rating plans
- Improper classification of accounts
- Inaccurate application of account classifications
- Anticompetitive practices

An application might state, for example, that the insured is an "optical goods wholesaler," for which the *Commercial Lines Manual* Classification Table does not contain a classification. The underwriter might know from experience that the ophthalmic industry has no wholesale companies. The manual offers an initial choice of either "Optical Goods Manufacturing" or "Optical Goods Stores." Footnotes to the first classification identify other, more specific classifications that address the manufacturing of contact lenses, eyeglass lenses, and photographic lenses. The underwriter should know that insufficient information has been provided to classify and price this account.

Underwriters need to be familiar with the rating process for individual rating plans and to have a working knowledge of rates and rate levels for specified classes. They do not, however, need to be familiar with the precise rate applicable to each classification. Therefore, an underwriter need not be familiar with the rate differentials between two closely related classifications. Still, having the ability to associate an approximate rate with each account is important. Since underwriters are responsible for assigning a rate suitable to the account, they must have a significant degree of familiarity with the loss exposure for which the rate has been prepared.

Classification is often considered to be a clerical task because it is delegated to the underwriting technicians who prepare the quotation or policy. This should not be the case. Underwriters should ensure that each account is properly classified since they usually have a better understanding of the insured's business than anyone else in the underwriting department. A large number of misclassified accounts or even a single misclassified account can cause an unprofitable book of business.

Factors Not Included in Rates

Many factors or attributes are not taken into consideration in the insurance pricing process. Some factors are not part of the rating process because they would apply to only a limited number of accounts or because they are relevant in only specific geographic locations. Other factors, though relevant to the exposure presented by the account, are too complex to be included.

Underwriters can often identify factors that indicate that an account is either superior or inferior for the premium being charged. The factors that can be quantified into objective criteria often become the basis for the insurer's underwriting guidelines. Subjective criteria can be valuable in an underwriting decision and in pricing through the operation of individual rating plans.

Individual Rating Plans

Individual rating plans provide insurers, and their underwriters, an avenue to tailor class rates to a specific account. The term "class rates" can be used in many contexts, but it usually means the loss costs that appear in the rating manual developed by an insurance advisory organization or the final rates that appear in insurer-developed rating manuals. In this context, a **class rate** for a particular classification reflects the aggregate loss experience of all accounts included in that classification. Most insurance rates are class rates. Exceptions, however, include **specific fire rates** developed by ISO. ISO field representatives visit each property and develop an individual advisory loss cost for that property. Another exception to class rates is the judgment rating approach used by marine and specialty underwriters. **Judgment rates** are developed by reviewing individual account characteristics and not from a classification plan that is backed with substantial loss experience.

Class rates are subject to inequity because the classifications used are often broadly defined. The broad classification definitions used in the ISO *Commercial Lines Manual* Classification Table are evident when they are compared to the classification scheme used by the North American Industry Classification System (NAICS), which was described in Chapter 3. Absolute rate equity could be achieved by developing a rate for each account or by creating a finely defined classification system. Absolute rate equity would be an expensive undertaking, and a highly defined classification plan might result in rates that are not actuarially credible. Individual rating plans serve as a compromise between a broadly defined classification plan that is easy and inexpensive to administer and individually developed rates for each account that would be difficult and costly to administer.

Individual rating plans use different approaches to tailoring the rate to an account. More than one individual rating plan might apply to an account. This section describes the following most frequently encountered individual rating plans:

- Experience rating
- Retrospective rating
- Schedule rating
- Individual risk premium modification
- Expense modification
- Participating

Experience Rating Plans

Experience rating plans adjust the class rate to reflect the insured's loss experience before the current policy period. The credit or debit calculated under the plan is applied to the applicable class rate. To be eligible, an account must have at least three years worth of loss experience, not including the immediate year prior to rating, and develop a specified minimum premium that varies by insurer.

Experience rating plans can be used for workers compensation, general liability, commercial auto liability, commercial auto physical damage, burglary, glass, theft, and credit insurance. In most states, underwriters have the option of using experience rating in any of the above lines of insurance except workers compensation, for which experience rating is often mandatory for eligible accounts. Underwriters should be aware that some state insurance departments have ruled that using an individual rating plan for some but not all eligible accounts is a form of unfair discrimination. These rulings have the effect of making experience rating plans compulsory for eligible accounts. They do, however, leave underwriters free to determine their own eligibility criteria as long as the criteria are applied to every account.

Experience Modification Factors

The experience modification factors shown below on an extract from an ACORD Workers Compensation Application indicate that the loss experience of this applicant has worsened in the past two years. The experience modification factor used for workers compensation policies is developed by the workers compensation bureau that has jurisdiction over the account. In other lines of business, insurers develop the experience modification factor used in premium determination.

PRIOR CARRIER INFORMATION/LOSS HISTORY

PROVIDE INFORMATION FOR THE PAST 5 YEARS AND USE THE REMARKS SECTION FOR LOSS DETAILS				LOSS RUN ATTACHED	

YEAR	CARRIER & POLICY NUMBER	ANNUAL PREMIUM	MOD	# CLAIMS	AMOUNT PAID	RESERVE
96/97	CO: Malvern Mutual POL#: WC 178 6013	$12,500	1.20	17	$17,000	Closed
97/98	CO: IIA Insurance Co. POL#: WC 71 27A	$13,500	1.38	21	$20,500	Closed
98/99	CO: Restrictive Indemnity POL#: WC 867 5309	$14,400	1.50	25	$24,800	$6.500
99/00	CO: Universal Mutual POL#: WC 711 7893	$17,700	1.55	30	$32,400	$10,500
	CO: POL#:					

© ACORD CORPORATION, 1980, USED WITH PERMISSION.

Experience rating plans enable insurers to apply price reductions and price increases as warranted by an account's loss experience. Although the determination of experience modification factors can be difficult for insureds to understand, most insureds do understand the relationship between their past losses and the premium they are being charged for the next policy term. Experience rating plans provide insureds a direct financial incentive to implement loss control measures.

Not all insureds are satisfied with the operation of or the result produced by experience rating plans. Insureds with improving loss experience often believe that the experience modification factor should only reflect the account's experience and not be minimized by a credibility factor. Experience rating plans use premium size at basic limits to determine a credibility factor. The larger the premium size, the more credibility the account's loss experience receives. Accounts that have relatively low premium size at basic limits develop an experience modification factor that reflects the average experience of all insureds more than their own loss experience.

Insureds who have made improvements in the prior policy term might assert that the experience modification factor is not responsive because it does not include data from the most recent year. By not including the most recent year in the experience rating modification factor determination, account loss control efforts are not recognized immediately in the insured's premium. Underwriters sometimes use retrospective rating plans, discussed later in this section, for those accounts that have made significant changes in their operations that would positively affect loss experience.

Underwriters sometimes use the experience rating modification factor as an index of the account's underwriting performance. The ACORD Commercial Insurance Application requests prior insurer information so that an experience rating modification factor can be calculated. Additionally, this application, as well as the ACORD Workers Compensation Application, requests the modification factor that was used by the insured's prior insurers. At a glance, the underwriter can tell if the account's loss experience is improving or deteriorating over time.

Retrospective Rating

Retrospective rating is an individual rating plan that uses the current policy year as the experience period to develop an experience modification factor. Under this plan, a provisional premium is charged at the beginning of the policy period. After the end of the policy period, the actual loss experience for that period is determined, and a final premium for that policy period is charged. The insured's premium is adjusted after the end of the policy period to cover losses and loss adjustment expenses incurred by the insured during the policy period, subject to specified minimum and maximum premiums. The retrospective rating formula can produce any combination of minimum and maximum premiums. However, there are four pre-selected plans, called "tabular plans," that vary in the fluctuation permitted in the final premium.

The important difference between experience rating and retrospective rating is that experience rating uses loss experience from prior policy periods in determining the premium for the current policy period. Retrospective rating uses the loss experience from the current policy period to determine the premium for the current policy period.

Unlike experience rating, retrospective rating is an option that must be elected in writing by the insured. Retrospective rating is usually reserved for large accounts and is primarily used for pricing workers compensation insurance. Retrospective rating can also be used for general liability, auto liability, auto physical damage, glass, and boiler and machinery insurance.

Retrospective Rating Formula[14]

The **retrospective rating formula** is an alternative to guaranteed-cost insurance pricing plans. The insured's premium can vary between a minimum and maximum premium, depending on the loss experience for that period. The retrospective rating formula developed by NCCI for workers compensation insurance is shown below:

Retrospective premium = (Basic premium + Converted losses) × Tax Multiplier

- The **basic premium** is the fixed cost element of the formula. The basic premium amount includes acquisition expenses, loss control services, premium audit, general administration of the insurance, an adjustment for limiting the retrospective premium to a stated maximum, and a provision for the insurer's profits and contingencies.

- **Converted losses** are the actual losses incurred increased by a factor (loss conversion factor) that reflects loss adjustment expenses.

- The **tax multiplier** enables the insurer to recapture expenses for licenses, fees, assesments, and taxes. This factor varies by state.

Numerous variations of this formula have been developed and are in use.

Retrospective rating plans appeal to insurers and insureds. Insurers market retrospective rating plans to accounts that might be considering self-insurance. Retrospective rating plans often allow the insured to pay the insurer only a small initial premium and make additional premium contributions as losses are incurred. Retrospective rating plans allow insureds to retain monies that would be spent on insurance premiums to serve the other business cash needs. Some insurers allow accounts even greater cash-flow flexibility by using a paid loss retrospective rating plan. A **paid loss retrospective plan** requires the insured to pay a deposit premium and make additional payments, usually monthly, as the insurer pays claims. Insureds are typically required to provide the insurer with a promissory note secured by an irrevocable letter of credit or with a surety bond that ensures payment of the balance of the premium.

While the retrospective rating formula is complex in its application, most insureds can visualize and understand the direct connection between current losses and current premiums. Retrospectively rated accounts are more likely to have a risk management program that encourages loss control to minimize premium fluctuations under the plan.

Schedule Rating and Individual Risk Premium Modification Plans

The **schedule rating plan** in liability insurance allows underwriters to modify the final premium to reflect factors that the class rate does not include. The **individual risk premium modification (IRPM)** plan achieves the same result in property insurance. The plans are very similar, and underwriters often refer to them both as "schedule rating."

When underwriting general liability coverage, for example, underwriters can apply the factors shown in Exhibit 5-1 to adjust the rate. The characteristics listed in the exhibit are attributes that are not considered in the development of the class rate but that could have an effect on the profitability of accounts. Schedule rating plans for other lines of business are similar to the general liability schedule rating table.

The IRPM plan allows underwriters to apply the same debits and credits to property rates. Most states limit the amount of the credits or debits that an underwriter can apply to an individual account. In some states, adjustments are limited to a debit or credit of 40 percent, and in other states the limit is a debit or credit of 25 percent.

The underwriter's judgment is of utmost importance when applying schedule rating and IRPM plans. Application of the debit or credit is based on the underwriter's experience in the line of business, the insured's loss experience, the insurer's underwriting policy, and any other relevant factors. Depending on the coverage and type of insured, the underwriter should emphasize the physical conditions and hazards of the premises and operations or management attitude toward loss control. In some lines, such as general liability, substantial emphasis is placed on subjective factors that include management's cooperation and training and supervision.

Schedule rating plans have been filed for optional use for commercial auto liability, commercial auto physical damage, general liability, glass, and burglary insurance. Generally, those insureds who are eligible to use experience rating are also eligible to use schedule rating. To become eligible for schedule rating, insureds must meet specified minimum premium amounts. As with experience rating, schedule rating must be used on every account that qualifies. Not every account will warrant a debit or credit. Some accounts will be documented with a zero percent modification factor.

Exhibit 5-1
Schedule Rating Table

The manual rates for the risk may also be modified in accordance with the following schedule rating table, subject to a maximum modification of 25%, to reflect such characteristics of the risk as are not reflected in its experience:

		CREDIT		DEBIT
A.	Location	5%	to	5%
	i. Exposure inside premises	5	to	5
	ii. Exposure outside premises	10	to	10
B.	Premises—condition, care	10	to	10
C.	Equipment—type, condition, care	10	to	10
D.	Classification peculiarities	10	to	10
E.	Employees—selection, training, supervision, experience	6	to	6
F.	Cooperation:			
	i. Medical facilities	2	to	2
	ii. Safety program	2	to	2

In addition to the schedule rating elements considered above, if the Expected Loss Ratio (ELR) underlying the company manual premium for the class is different than the actual ELR for the risk, multiply the otherwise chargeable premium (after experience modification) by the following expense variation factor:

$$\text{Expense variation factor} = \frac{\text{ELR underlying the company manual premium}}{\text{Actual ELR for the risk}}$$

Includes copyrighted material of Insurance Services Office, Inc., with its permission. Copyright, Insurance Services Office, Inc., 1990.

Expense Modification

Expense modification is a rating plan that modifies the expense portion of an insured's rate to reflect the actual cost of providing coverage to that insured. Under these plans, the underwriters use their judgment to determine whether the account is expected to have fewer expenses than the average account associated with it. Account expense savings are usually derived from reduced commissions to agents or brokers and reduced loss control costs. Expense modification can be used in conjunction with schedule and experience rating plans. Expense modification plans are not permitted in every state. Where they are permitted, expense modification plans must be filed with state insurance regulators.

Agents and brokers are sometimes willing to reduce their commission rate to make the premium charged an account more competitive. If, for example, the normal commission rate for a line of business is 15 percent, the agent or broker might accept only 10 percent if it means writing the account. The savings in commission expense can be passed along to the insured through the expense modification plan. This reduction in commission is *not* considered to be rebating because the rate reduction is authorized by a filing with the state insurance department and is based on specific expense savings.

Rebating[15]

Rebating is the act of giving or offering some benefit to a customer other than those described in the policy in an effort to induce a customer to purchase insurance. Rebating is a violation of the law in all states except Florida and California.

Expense savings can also be achieved when the insured is willing to cooperate fully with the insurer's loss control efforts. As discussed in Chapter 3, loss control reports can be expensive to obtain, and loss control recommendations expensive to monitor or enforce. Underwriters are often able to reward accounts that collaborate with the insurer on loss control through expense modification plans.

Expense modification plans should be used with discretion. Underwriters might envision expense savings that do not materialize. Some underwriters use expense modification plans strictly as an approach to developing a more competitive rate without regard to the limited expense loading present in competitive rates. Underwriters using expense modification plans should determine whether the expense modification afforded an account could be justified during an underwriting audit.

Participating Plans

Participating plans, like retrospective rating plans, use the loss experience of an insured for the *current* policy period to adjust the premium at the end of the policy period. That adjustment is done, in most cases, by using a graded or sliding scale dividend that varies with the size of the premium and loss ratio. The dividend is paid from premiums that remain after all losses and expenses have been paid. Dividends are not guaranteed, but in practice participating plans usually do pay a dividend to accounts to which the plan applies. As a requirement of the plan, the insurer's board of directors must approve the payment of dividends to accounts included in the plan. Participating plans can usually be applied also to accounts that are schedule and experience rated.

Participating plans are generally used with large accounts that have better-than-average loss experience. Some participating plans require that the account develop a substantial minimum premium, such as $100,000. Insurers might have several participating plans available with tiered minimum premiums to accommodate more accounts and at appropriate dividend levels. Underwriters sometimes refer to participating plans as "one-way retros" because the accounts receive the dividend when losses and expenses are less than expected but are not penalized when losses and expenses exceed expectations. Usually, participating plans are used for workers compensation insurance, but they can be used to price other lines of business as well. Underwriters can use participating plans with accounts that are already priced using schedule and experience rating.

Composite Rating

Composite rating is an optional pricing approach in which a premium base other than the one specified in the rating manual is used to price an entire account. Composite rating serves as an administrative convenience for the insurer and the insured. For example, instead of using the various premium bases for a fuel oil dealer's account, the underwriter and the insured might agree to use the general liability premium basis of gallons delivered as the premium base for the entire account. In this example, the insured knows the insurance costs associated with every gallon of fuel oil delivered and can adjust the retail price accordingly. Many accounts want to have a consolidated premium base that enables them to readily determine and pass along insurance costs to customers.

Insurers do not have to perform mid-term pricing on composite-rated accounts because changes in exposure (for example, gallons delivered in the above example) will be discovered by premium audit at the end of the policy term. While a fuel oil dealer would usually be required to submit information on any autos added during the policy term, the underwriter will not have to have these autos rated to determine a premium for the remainder of the policy term. Rather, the increased exposure these autos present will be rated at the end of the policy term when the total amount of fuel oil delivered is known.

Composite rating differs from other pricing plans in that the insured receives no price advantage by being composite rated. An account's premium under composite rating normally should not be substantially different than if it were determined without composite rating. Exhibit 5-2 shows how the premium for the fuel oil dealer might be determined using composite rating.

Exhibit 5-2

Composite Rating Example

Step 1—Calculate the premium for each individual coverage under the plan, using the class rates, premium basis, and experience and schedule rating plans for that coverage.

COVERAGE	PREMIUM BASE	PREMIUM
Auto liability	Specified auto	$ 46,000
General liability	1,000 gallons	30,000
Total		$ 76,000

Step 2—Determine the new premium base.

Fuel Oil Dealer and Underwriter agreed to each use 1,000 gallons of fuel oil delivered as the premium basis for the entire account. Last year, Fuel Oil Dealer delivered 1,200,000 gallons of oil.

1,200,000 ÷ 1,000 = 1,200.

Step 3—Calculate the composite rate.

$76,000 ÷ 1,200 = $63.33 per 1,000 gallons of fuel oil delivered

The composite rate can be adjusted. The composite rate is normally recalculated annually. The insurer or the insured, however, can request that the composite rate be recalculated if the class rates change or if the mix of the insured's exposures changes significantly.

Not all insureds are eligible for composite rating. Most insurers require eligible accounts to meet a specified minimum premium requirement and that there be a practical justification for using this approach.

Summary

Actuaries and underwriters each have a role in insurance pricing. Actuaries perform ratemaking, in which rates for each classification in the insured's book of business are determined. Underwriters apply those rates by performing the mechanics of classification and rating. In many instances, underwriters modify the rate to reflect the loss exposures presented by the account. Pricing insurance is a challenging task for underwriters and actuaries because the underlying costs, primarily losses, are not known when the insurance is priced.

The law of large numbers is the mathematical principle that serves as the foundation for insurance pricing. This law states that the accuracy of loss predictions increases as the number of exposure units increases. In order for increasing the number of exposure units to likewise increase the predictability of losses, the exposure units should have similar loss potential and be independent of one another. Moreover, insurers seek to insure losses that are fortuitous, that can definitely be measured in time and place of occurrence, and that are economically feasible to insure.

Insurance pricing is regulated to ensure insurer solvency and ensure equity. The objectives of rate regulation are that rates be adequate, not excessive, and not unfairly discriminatory. Within these constraints, insurers have flexibility in setting the price for their insurance products. Insurance regulators rely on competition in the insurance marketplace to control insurance pricing. In circumstances in which competition does not control pricing or in which competition becomes destructive, state insurance regulators intervene. Additionally, state insurance regulators want insurers to set rates so that insurance is available and affordable. Availability and affordability problems usually indicate that the insurance marketplace is not administering prices as it should and that regulatory intervention is needed.

Underwriters are responsible for ensuring that accounts are properly classified and rated. Account classification means evaluating an account's characteristics to determine what set of manual rates should apply. Rating usually means applying the manual rate to the number of exposure units applicable to the account.

Individual rating plans enable underwiters to make adjustments to manual premiums. Experience rating plans and retrospective rating plans adjust the insured's premium to reflect the insured's actual loss experience. Unlike experience rating, which uses three years worth of previous loss experience to modify the premium for the current policy period, retrospective rating plans adjust current-year premiums to reflect current-year loss experience. Schedule rating and individual rate premium modification plans allow underwriters to adjust rates using account characteristics that usually are not directly recognized in the manual rate. Expense modification plans permit a price adjustment when the expenses associated with writing an account are anticipated to be lower than those contemplated in the rate. Individual rate modification plans make the rating process flexible and allow underwriters to adjust prices to reflect current conditions and the level of competition in the insurance marketplace.

Insurers sometimes find the process of rating each exposure separately for a large account burdensome. Most insurance forms and rating plans, by design, assume that separate insurance premiums must be developed for each line of insurance. Composite rating solves that problem by converting several exposures to a single rate and a single rating basis.

Chapter Notes

1. Stephen M. Stigler, *The History of Statistics: Measurement of Uncertainty before 1900* (Cambridge, MA: Harvard University Press, 1986), p. 65.

2. Robert J. Gibbons, George E. Rejda, and Michael W. Elliott, *Insurance Perspectives* (Malvern, PA: American Institute for Chartered Property Casualty Underwriters, 1992), p. 10.

3. J. J. Launie, J. Finley Lee, Norman A. Baglini, *Principles of Property and Liability Underwriting*, 3d ed. (Malvern, PA: Insurance Institute of America, 1986), p. 244.

4. Constance M. Luthardt, Barry D. Smith, and Eric A. Wiening, *Property and Liability Insurance Principles* (Malvern, PA: Insurance Institute of America, 1999), pp. 1-8 through 1-9.

5. Kathleen Heald Ettlinger, Karen L. Hamilton, and Gregory Krohm, *State Insurance Regulation* (Malvern, PA: Insurance Institute of America, 1995), pp. 65-69. This section of *State Insurance Regulation* describes the history of rate regulation.

6. The Sherman Act does, however, apply to boycott, coercion, or intimidation.

7. Ettlinger, Hamilton, and Krohm, p. 68.

8. In 1989, ISO announced its decision to stop providing final rates to its members.

9. In a referendum, California voters passed Proposition 103 reduced rates and changed the way California regulated rates. A significant issue that came out of this change was the debate of what constituted a fair rate of return for insurers. The California court determined that 10 percent was a fair rate of return.

10. The Florida Department of Insurance annually establishes profit levels by line of business that may be used in rate filings.

11. Ettlinger, Hamilton, and Krohm, p. 64.

12. Ettlinger, Hamilton, and Krohm, pp. 3 and 43.

13. National Association of Insurance Commissioners, *Market Conduct Examiners' Handbook* (Kansas City, MO: NAIC, 1994), p. V-1.

14. National Council on Compensation Insurance, *Retrospective Rating Plan Manual for Workers Compensation and Employers Liability* (effective October 1, 1993, Part Two), p. 4.

15. Ettlinger, Hamilton, and Krohm, p. 199.

Index